Don't Teach! Let Me Learn!

Inquiry Learning in English

Nina Crosby and
Elizabeth Marten

HAWKER BROWNLOW
EDUCATION

The following topics are included in the
Don't teach! Let me learn! series:

Inquiry learning in Humanities: Art – Poetry – Shakespeare – Music – Architecture – Chefs, cooking and food fashion and design – Inventors and inventions.

Inquiry learning in English: Mysteries – Mythology – Fairytales, Fables and legends – The supernatural – Adventure – Dreams – Superstition – Monsters – Fantasy.

Inquiry learning in Life Science: Arachnids – Frogs and toads – The animal world – Monkeys – Fish and undersea life – Robots and computers – Science fiction – Astronomy.

Cover design by Lauren Mills

Originally published by
D.O.K. Publishers, Inc.

Republished in Australia by
HAWKER BROWNLOW
•
E D U C A T I O N

P.O. Box 8580, Heatherton
Victoria 3202, Australia
Phone: (03) 8558 2444 Fax: (03) 8558 2400
Toll Free Ph: 1800 33 4603 Fax: 1800 15 0445
Website: http://www.hbe.com.au
Email: orders@hbe.com.au

© 1982 D.O.K. Publishers, Inc.
© 1990 Hawker Brownlow Education
© 2006 Reprinted Hawker Brownlow Education

All Rights Reserved
Printed in Australia

Code: HB6487
ISBN: 1 74101 648 7
0206

Contents

Don't teach! Let me learn!

Don't teach! Let me learn! is a series of multi-disciplinary units of instruction capitalising on student interest and spotlighting necessary skill development. These units are intended to extend and enrich the school curriculum by broadening the topics and providing experiences to help students become more skillful in interpretation of materials, application of independent study skills and stimulation of creative thinking.

Activities in unit packs may be used as a supplement to the regular curriculum. Each unit may be used as a total classroom study or with individual students exhibiting a special interest. Portions of the unit or single activities may be selected to enrich a specific lesson or to extend the work of a single student or group. Likewise, the entire unit may be used for a specialised, intense study on an independent basis.

Nina E. Crosby   Elizabeth H. Marten

To the teacher

Don't teach! let me learn! was developed by practising educators to provide a vehicle for reaching and motivating the middle-years student. Each unit allows the student a wide variety of ways to learn and may be used in total or in part as needed to supplement the regular school curriculum.

The level of difficulty of each individual activity, based on Bloom's Taxonomy of Cognitive Thinking, is indicated on the matrix chart at the start of every unit and on each individual activity card. Activities are also classified by subject area. See the Bloom's Taxonomy objective key on the following page to gain a clear understanding of the activity levels. This will aid you in making choices consistent with your goals and objectives.

Also included for your use are suggestions for record keeping. Student logs allow students to keep records of their progress and provide a means for you to evaluate or assess their progress.

Each unit of study contains many activity choices providing stimulation and variation for your students. Activity titles and objectives are identified. Activity language is directed to the student. Activities are complete rather than dependent upon one another, therefore, they may be used to meet your classroom needs.

Bloom's Taxonomy objective key

O Remembering   O Understanding   O Applying
O Analysing   O Evaluating   O Creating

Level	Goals	Activity design
Remembering	Ability to recall facts, concepts or principles.	List, recognise, label, locate, describe, define, observe.
Understanding	Ability to translate or interpret information. A grasp of meaning, intent and relationship is demonstrated in oral, written or non-verbal communication.	Explain, demonstrate, show, paraphrase, experiment, discover, illustrate, infer, predict.
Applying	Ability to apply previously acquired knowledge or information to a new or concrete situation.	Organise, collect, summarise, order, record, classify, model, construct, relate, generalise, transfer, code, draw, reconstruct.
Analysing	Ability to break down material into its components so that organisational structure may be understood.	Take away, put together, formulate, deduce, compare, contrast, combine, solve, discriminate, take apart, fill.
Evaluating	Ability to make judgments based on evidence and determine the value of material based on definite criteria.	Appraise, interpret, judge, validate, justify, criticise, assess, decide, defend, rate.
Creating	Ability to analyse the parts and put them together to form a new whole.	Create, imagine, suppose, predict, assume, translate, hypothesise, design, derive.

Student activity record

Student: _____

Teacher: _____

Topic: _____

Activity number	Comments	Date begun	Date completed

Mysteries

Mysteries

Activity	Remembering	Understanding	Applying	Analysing	Evaluating	Creating
1			x	x		
2	x	x	x			
3		x			x	x
4	x	x				
5		x	x	x	x	
6				x	x	
7				x		x
8				x	x	x
9	x	x		x		
10			x	x		
11	x	x		x		
12		x	x	x		
13				x		x
14	x	x				
15	x	x	x			x
16		x		x		
17				x	x	
18			x	x	x	
19	x					
20	x	x	x			
21			x			x
22		x	x			
23				x	x	x
24				x		x
25		x				x

Mysteries

Activity	Remembering	Understanding	Applying	Analysing	Evaluating	Creating
26		x		x		x
27	x	x				
28	x	x		x	x	
29	x	x	x			
30				x		
31				x	x	
32	x	x	x			
33		x	x		x	x
34				x	x	
35		x		x	x	x
36				x		x
37	x	x				
38	x	x	x			
39					x	x
40		x		x	x	
41				x	x	x
42					x	x
43			x	x		
44			x	x		x
45			x	x		
46		x		x		
47		x		x		
48				x		
49				x		x
50		x	x	x		x

1. Mystery comparisons

Mysteries

Choose two good mystery stories you have read. What did they have in common? What were the differences? What techniques did the authors use to hold your attention?

O R	O U	⊙ Ap
⊙ An	O E	O C

2. Favourite game

Mysteries

Cluedo is a game that challenges its players to solve mysteries by examining clues. Play this game with others in your group.

⊙ R	⊙ U	⊙ Ap
O An	O E	O C

3. Mystery codes

Mysteries

Secret codes are often used in mystery stories. Develop your own secret code. Send a message to a friend. See if your friend can decode the message by figuring out your code.

O R	⊙ U	O Ap
O An	⊙ E	⊙ C

4. Spooky words

Mysteries

Make a list of mystery words or terms that give you a spooky feeling. Examples: eerie, weird, ghostly. See how many you can think of.

⊙ R	⊙ U	O Ap
O An	O E	O C

5. Old favourites

Mysteries

Nancy Drew and The Hardy Boys are two famous mystery series. Read several of these books. Compare and contrast them. Why do you believe they are so popular?

O R	⊙ U	⊙ Ap
⊙ An	⊙ E	O C

6. Television mystery

Mysteries

Many mystery shows are broadcast on television. Watch one of these shows. Write a critique of the show. Tell how the show could have been improved.

O R	O U	O Ap
⊙ An	⊙ E	O C

7. Mystery patterns

Most mystery stories follow a similar pattern. There is an introduction that sets the stage. The second section builds the suspense and provides clues. Finally, the author solves the mystery. Try your skill at being a mystery writer. Create your own exciting mystery story.

○ R	○ U	○ Ap
⊙ An	○ E	⊙ C

8. Ending comparisons

Read a mystery story. Stop when you think you have enough clues to solve the mystery. Write your own ending. Now finish reading the story. How did your ending compare with that of the author? If your ending was quite different, give reasons for these differences.

○ R	○ U	○ Ap
⊙ An	⊙ E	⊙ C

9. Private eye

Many mystery stories might be classified as detective fiction. Trace the history of detective fiction stories from the mid 1700s to the present. How have the story ideas changed over the years? Why do you think these changes have occurred? Find out what the word 'genre' means.

⊙ R	⊙ U	○ Ap
⊙ An	○ E	○ C

10. Comparisons

Read at least one Sherlock Holmes story. Compare Holmes and Watson to modern detectives. Why do you think Holmes's stories have remained popular over the years? What media forms have they taken?

○ R	○ U	⊙ Ap
⊙ An	○ E	○ C

11. Poe's prose

Mysteries

Read several selections written by Edgar Allan Poe. Record the clues/time tabling/tracking that lead to logical deduction.

⊙ R   ⊙ U   O Ap
⊙ An   O E   O C

12. How many?

Mysteries

Write the word 'mysterious' at the top of your paper. Make as many words from these letters as possible.

O R   ⊙ U   ⊙ Ap
⊙ An   O E   O C

13. Combine ideas

Mysteries

Consider these elements: a haunted house, an old man with a beard, a bloody knife, a can of baked beans and a dog.
Write a mystery story to include each element.

O R   O U   O Ap
⊙ An   O E   ⊙ C

14. Media mysteries

Mysteries

Radio, movies and television have made famous Miss Marple, Father Dowling and many others. List as many famous detectives and mystery solvers as you can.
Find the origin of each.

⊙ R   ⊙ U   O Ap
O An   O E   O C

15. Life and times

Mysteries

Edgar Allan Poe is one of the best known American writers of detective fiction. Research his life. What things in his background might have contributed to his mystery writing ability?

⊙ R   ⊙ U   ⊙ Ap
O An   O E   ⊙ C

16. Gothic ghosts

Mysteries

Gothic novels are tales of terror. What is a Gothic novel? What elements does it have? Read one from your library. Why do you think they are so popular? How many Gothic novels written by women can you find?

O R   ⊙ U   O Ap
⊙ An   O E   O C

17. Elementary, my dear Watson

Sherlock Holmes, the detective character created by Arthur Conan Doyle, inspired the comment, 'He is more than a book – he is the spirit of a town and a time'. Explain what is meant by this statement.

O R   O U   O Ap
⊙ An   ⊙ E   O C

18. Finger printing

Fingerprints are often clues that lead to crime solution. Fingerprint yourself and others in your group. Can you make positive identifications without looking at the names? What other physical characteristics can be used for identification? When did fingerprinting become a standard part of crime detection?

O R   O U   ⊙ Ap
⊙ An   ⊙ E   O C

19. Mystery words

These words might be used in mystery or detective stories. Search out their meanings.

- Interrogation
- Forgery
- Extortion
- Racketeer
- Fraud
- Vagrant
- Probation
- Ballistics
- Ransom
- Saboteur
- Espionage
- Hoax

⊙ R   O U   O Ap
O An   O E   O C

20. Famous figures

Can you think of a fictional character that represents each of these groups or agencies mentioned in activity 22? Make a chart of famous figures from each agency. Do you know of a real situation in which any of these agencies were involved?

⊙ R   ⊙ U   ⊙ Ap
O An   O E   O C

21. Figure it out

Choose one method of communicating with a code. (You may want to use your own code). Write a mystery story using the code you have selected to help the characters solve the mystery.

| O R | O U | ⊙ Ap |
| O An | O E | ⊙ C |

22. Police report

Police and other law enforcement agencies solve 'mysteries'. Investigate each of the following law enforcement agencies: ASIC, Scotland Yard, Canadian Mounted Police. Summarise information you gather about each.

| O R | ⊙ U | ⊙ Ap |
| O An | O E | O C |

23. Mystery moves

Make a 'ghostly' mobile. Design symbols to create a look of mystery. Construct a mobile to be suspended from the ceiling. Perhaps your mobile could represent a story you have read.

| O R | O U | O Ap |
| ⊙ An | ⊙ E | ⊙ C |

24. Play it again

Make a mystery board game. Perhaps you will want to use ideas you have taken from a mystery book you have read.

| O R | O U | O Ap |
| ⊙ An | O E | ⊙ C |

25. Look closely

Make a word search using mysterious or spooky words. Let other members of the group solve your word search mystery.

| O R | ⊙ U | O Ap |
| O An | O E | ⊙ C |

26. And other tales

'The Tattooed Potato' is a mystery spoof! Read the book. Note the sequence of development repeated in each situation or experience. Write a sequel chapter with another experience for these super characters.

| O R | ⊙ U | O Ap |
| ⊙ An | O E | ⊙ C |

27. Mysterious messages

There are a number of 'mysterious' ways to communicate. Investigate one or more of the following codes or sets of signals used for communication.

• Semaphore flags
• Sign language for the deaf
• Morse code
• Flag hoists

⊙ R   ⊙ U   ○ Ap
○ An   ○ E   ○ C

28. Stereotypes

What are the similarities or differences between the way female and male characters are depicted in detective stories? What characteristics are these characters given? Compare at least three stories and look at the main characters as well as the minor ones. Make a list of similarities and differences.

⊙ R   ⊙ U   ○ Ap
⊙ An   ⊙ E   ○ C

29. Now you see it!

The juice of a lemon can be used as invisible ink. Write a message using a toothpick dipped in lemon juice. By warming the paper in a moderate oven, you can make the message appear. Try it! Find some other ways to make invisible ink. Try them, too!

⊙ R   ⊙ U   ⊙ Ap
○ An   ○ E   ○ C

30. World conditions

Good mysteries remain timeless in many respects, but authors usually show the state of the world at the time. Find out what 'Roman Noir' is and when this style was used. Look at the works of several authors from different periods in history. Can you find evidence of political or economic situations? Compare to the actual time period.

○ R   ○ U   ○ Ap
⊙ An   ○ E   ○ C

31. Let's compare

Select two mysteries you have read and especially liked. Identify the villain in each. List each of their characteristics or attributes. Using your lists, compare and contrast the villains.

○ R	○ U	○ Ap
⊙ An	⊙ E	○ C

32. Women's work

Make a list of women writers who were working in the 1700s, 1800s and 1900s. What type of stories were written in these different eras? List book titles and genre after each author.

⊙ R	⊙ U	⊙ Ap
○ An	○ E	○ C

33. Ghostly Gothic

In activity 16 you found out about Gothic novels. In small groups, write a 'modern' Gothic story. Don't leave out any of the Gothic elements.

○ R	⊙ U	⊙ Ap
○ An	⊙ E	⊙ C

34. TV mysteries

Make a list of mysteries shown on television for a week. Compare these programs to the other types of shows. What do you note about the popularity of mysteries? What generalisations about viewer preferences can you make?

○ R	○ U	○ Ap
⊙ An	⊙ E	○ C

35. Pen name

S.S. Van Dine, mystery writer in the 1920s, had great appeal to the reading audience. This was not his real name. Who was Van Dine? Why do you think he selected this pen name? Can you think of a suitable pen name to use as you write?

○ R	⊙ U	○ Ap
⊙ An	⊙ E	⊙ C

36. News views

Check the local newspaper and/or local police department. Are there any unsolved crimes or local mysteries in your community? Give a summary of known information. Suggest a possible solution to the 'mystery'.

○ R	○ U	○ Ap
⊙ An	○ E	⊙ C

37. E.S.P.

People with psychic abilities, particularly clairvoyance, are sometimes called upon to solve mysteries for police departments. Explain the terms 'psychic' and 'clairvoyant'. Explain how these abilities might solve a mystery. Give examples of the use of psychics in real life.

⦿ R	⦿ U	○ Ap
○ An	○ E	○ C

38. Queen of the golden age

Agatha Christie is one of the best known mystery writers of all time. Research her life and work. Make a chart to show titles of her works and how many versions there have been. Which of her books have been made into movies? Analyse any that you have seen or read for the golden age characteristics outlined in activity 48.

⦿ R	⦿ U	⦿ Ap
○ An	○ E	○ C

39. Favourites

Survey adults in your neighbourhood to find out what kinds of books they read. Make a graph or chart to show the results of your survey. What generalisations can you make about your respondents' preferences? How do mysteries fit into your readers' preferences? You may wish to repeat the survey with your classmates and compare results.

○ R	○ U	○ Ap
○ An	⦿ E	⦿ C

40. Logical thought

What are the differences between inductive and deductive thinking? With these two methods of reasoning in mind, read or recall several mystery stories. What type of reasoning is used to solve the mystery in each case? Give examples from the story to support your judgment.

○ R	⦿ U	○ Ap
⦿ An	⦿ E	○ C

41. Create a villain

Consider those characteristics we usually associate with villains. Brainstorm a list of such traits. Now create 'the villain' of all times. Make a drawing of your villain to show physical traits. List the personality traits. Now swap villains with a classmate.

O R	O U	O Ap
⊙ An	⊙ E	⊙ C

42. Group story

Write a collaborative mystery story. A small group or even a whole class can work together to develop a mystery. Define characters and the setting first. Then decide on a sequence of events, the crime and other important details. Take care to develop your plot logically.

O R	O U	O Ap
O An	⊙ E	⊙ C

43. Which is which

Mysteries, detective stories and suspense stories are all similar and in some ways related. Yet each type is different and has its own set of distinct characteristics. Make a comparison of the three story types. How are they alike? How are they different? You may want to chart your data to make the comparison easier.

O R	O U	⊙ Ap
⊙ An	O E	O C

44. News notes

Real life happenings are sometimes the basis for detective, suspense or mystery novels. Scan your local paper for news stories that have an air of mystery about them. As you read them, notice the language the journalists use to tell the story. What words or phrases do they use to make the story more compelling? Select one article and use it as the basis for a mystery novel of your own.

O R	O U	⊙ Ap
⊙ An	O E	⊙ C

45. Famous detectives

Compare these 'detectives'. Look at physical descriptions, character traits, actions and methods of solving crimes. How are they alike? How are they different? In each case, what characteristics do you think have made them real to readers?

• Sir Arthur Conan Doyle's Sherlock Holmes
• Agatha Christie's Miss Marple
• Earl Stanley Gardner's Perry Mason

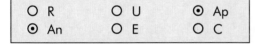

46. The first

In April, 1841, Edgar Allan Poe's *The Murders in the Rue Morgue* appeared as a short story in *Graham's Magazine*. This was considered to be the first published mystery. Read the story. What elements of mystery are contained in the story? How does it compare to modern mystery stories?

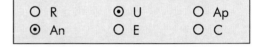

47. News notes

Real life happenings are sometimes the basis for detective, suspense or mystery novels. Scan your local paper for news stories that have an air of mystery about them. As you read through them, notice the language the journalists use to tell the story. What words or phrases do they use to make the story more compelling? Select one and use it as the basis for a mystery novel of your own.

48. The golden age

The golden age of mystery writing was the period between World War I and World War II. Good detective story writers of the time followed certain guidelines. Write your own story following these rules:

a. All clues must be available to both the fictional detective and the reader so that the reader has a chance to outsmart the detective.
b. The crime must be important so that it merits solving.
c. The criminal is introduced early in the development of the story.
d. The solution must be based on reason.

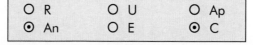

49. Biography bonus

Choose one of these mystery/detective/suspense novelists. Make a thorough search of facts about the author you select. Write a biographical sketch to include the information you have found. Make your character sketch appeal to your readers. Keep it interesting.

- Arthur Conan Doyle
- Mary Roberts Rinehart
- Wilkie Collins
- G.K. Chesterton
- Ruth Rendell
- Gaston Leroux

- P.D. James
- Raymond Chandler
- Charles Dickens
- John Le Carré
- Agatha Christie
- Dorothy L. Sayers

Mythology

Mythology

Activity	Remembering	Understanding	Applying	Analysing	Evaluating	Creating
1				x	x	x
2		x	x	x	x	
3	x	x	x			
4				x	x	
5		x	x	x		
6	x	x				
7				x		x
8		x		x		x
9	x	x	x	x		
10				x	x	
11				x	x	x
12	x			x	x	x
13		x	x	x		
14	x	x				x
15	x	x	x	x		x
16	x	x	x			
17				x		x
18	x	x	x	x		x
19	x	x	x	x		x
20				x		x

Mythology

Activity	Remembering	Understanding	Applying	Analysing	Evaluating	Creating
21			x	x		
22	x	x	x			
23				x		x
24	x	x	x			
25				x	x	
26	x	x				
27	x	x	x			
28				x		x
29	x	x				
30				x		x
31	x	x	x			
32				x	x	x
33	x	x	x			
34				x	x	
35	x	x				
36				x	x	x
37	x	x	x	x		x
38				x		x
39				x		x
40	x	x	x	x		x

23 *Don't teach! Let me learn!* HB6487

1. Feelings

Great myths deal with deep human problems and emotions. Write an original myth to solve a problem or demonstrate an emotion which you feel is important. Classify your myth. Give reasons.

O R	O U	O Ap
⊙ An	⊙ E	⊙ C

2. Trojan victory

Read several accounts of the Trojan War. Make a model or diagram of the Trojan horse. How was the horse used in battle? What trickery led to a war time victory? What qualities of the stories qualify them as myths?

O R	⊙ U	⊙ Ap
⊙ An	⊙ E	O C

3. Mythological figures

The following mythical characters were quite similar in different cultures. Identify each character by culture and the qualities attributed to this figure: Ceres, Demeter, Diana, Artemis, Isis.

⊙ R	⊙ U	⊙ Ap
O An	O E	O C

4. Some of each

Many mythological characters have both human and animal qualities. Explain how this was true of the Gorgons.

O R	O U	O Ap
⊙ An	⊙ E	O C

5. Paving the way

The exploration of Mexico by Hernando Cortez was made easy because of a myth. Explain how the beliefs of the Aztec people paved the way for Cortez's exploration.

O R	⊙ U	⊙ Ap
⊙ An	O E	O C

6. Mortals and Immortals

Briefly summarise the story involving these characters: Rhea and Kronus; Demeter, Persephone and Hades; Cassandra and Paris; Penthesilia; Amphitrite; Hel.

⊙ R	⊙ U	O Ap
O An	O E	O C

7. Myths by category

Myths may be divided into categories by type. These major types include nature myths, semi historical myths, myths of explanation, creation myths and myths about the world of the dead. Find out what characteristics are necessary to classify myths by category. Read a sampling of myths. Explain which category they should be classified in and why.

O R	O U	O Ap
⊙ An	O E	⊙ C

8. Beginnings of Greek literature

Homer is the author credited with beginning Greek literature. He is known for his epic poems *The Iliad* and *The Odyssey*. Read the editions with which you are comfortable. Discuss the hero. From the description of the Cyclops, draw a picture of the creature.

O R	⊙ U	O Ap
⊙ An	O E	⊙ C

9. Myriad of characters

Make a chart to show mythological characters from different cultures who represent the same idea or quality.

	Greek	Roman	Norse	Egyptian	Hindu
Love					
Light					
War					
Nature					
Wisdom					
Fire					
Other					

⊙ R	⊙ U	⊙ Ap
⊙ An	O E	O C

10. Lion strength

Unnatural feats of strength, skill or cunning are important features of myths. Discuss some of the super hero feats you discover.
For example, read about Atlanta or Achilles.

○ R	○ U	○ Ap
⊙ An	⊙ E	○ C

11. Create a creature

Create a mythological creature. Describe your creature. Illustrate your description. Use this creature as a character in an original myth.

○ R	○ U	○ Ap
⊙ An	⊙ E	⊙ C

12. Pandora's box

Read about Pandora. List the 'things' which Pandora lost. Choose one of these 'things'. Write an essay explaining how our world would be different without this 'thing'.

⊙ R	○ U	○ Ap
⊙ An	⊙ E	⊙ C

13. Commercial name game

Can you think of commercial products which have been given names from mythology? How does its name reflect the myth? Explain. Examples: Mars Bars, Apollo, Nike, Artemis.

○ R	⊙ U	⊙ Ap
⊙ An	○ E	○ C

14. Diorama

Where is Mount Olympus? What is its significance in mythology? Make a three-dimensional model showing the mountain and its gods and goddesses.

⊙ R	⊙ U	○ Ap
○ An	○ E	⊙ C

15. Moon myths

Are there any modern myths or superstitions about the moon? Are there any actual phenomena that could be attributed to the moon? Create a poster of moon facts and fancies.

⊙ R	⊙ U	⊙ Ap
⊙ An	○ E	⊙ C

16. Ancient connection

Many of the words we use today come from the names of mythical figures. For example, 'hygiene' is taken from Hygeia goddess of health; 'psyche' is taken from Psyche, the Greek personification of the human soul. Make a word list of as many examples as you can find including definitions and add to this list whenever you discover another example.

⊙ R   ⊙ U   ⊙ Ap
○ An   ○ E   ○ C

17. Make believe

Try your hand at writing 'fun' myths. Possible story starters:
- Why the kangaroo has a long tail and a pouch ...
- Why the tail of the lyrebird resembles the ancient stringed lyre ...
- Why the platypus has a snout shaped like a duck's bill, a tail like a beaver, and webbed feet with long claws ...

○ R   ○ U   ○ Ap
⊙ An   ○ E   ⊙ C

18. Lunar cycles

All cultures have worshipped the moon; some cultures even used to plant and harvest crops by the different phases of the moon. Research at least three different cultures and create a short book on moon lore. Have any mythological figures been related to the moon? Are there any modern myths or superstitions related to the moon? Are there any actual phenomena that could be attributed to the moon? Create a poster of moon facts and fancies.

⊙ R   ⊙ U   ⊙ Ap
⊙ An   ○ E   ⊙ C

19. Mother earth – Mother nature

'Ge' and 'Gaia' were the Greek names given to the Earth. Each culture has created myths and goddess figures related to the Earth. Find out as many names and characteristics attributed to the Earth as you can. Are there any similarities between cultures? Make a book which features this information in words and pictures.

⊙ R   ⊙ U   ⊙ Ap
⊙ An   ○ E   ⊙ C

20. Modern mythology

Myths have historically been used to explain the unexplained. Consider the world in which you live. What phenomenon can you identify that people in general do not understand? Choose one of these areas. Write a modern myth to explain the idea.

O R	O U	O Ap
⊙ An	O E	⊙ C

21. Differences

Both myths and legends are story forms that are used to explain a mysterious or unexplained event. How are the two story forms different? Read one of each and compare. Which one seems based in history? Which seems more related to the supernatural?

O R	O U	⊙ Ap
⊙ An	O E	O C

22. Stealing the sun

A Korean myth tells of the King of the Land of Gamag Nara planning to steal the sun. For what reasons was this necessary? What was the plan? What natural phenomenon was this myth attempting to explain? What is the scientific explanation we accept today?

⊙ R	⊙ U	⊙ Ap
O An	O E	O C

23. Human/animal synthesis

Ancient Egyptian myths featured gods and goddesses who had human bodies and heads of animals. Make a poster to show these various characters. What domain did they oversee or control? Be sure to include the Sphinx, Anubis, Set and Horus. You may also add others.

O R	O U	O Ap
⊙ An	O E	⊙ C

24. Places and names

Hundreds of mythological names have been given to continents and countries. For example, Asia, Africa, Europe, Holland, China, Scotland, Ireland. Try to find as many of these as you can and mark the name and origin of the name on a map of the world.

⊙ R	⊙ U	⊙ Ap
○ An	○ E	○ C

25. King Arthur mythology

King Arthur's drawing of the sword from the stone is thought to be the remainder of an ancient myth. It is said to be symbolic of the inventor of iron who freed the ore from the rock found in nature. What elements of the King Arthur tale indicate this might be a true assumption? Why might stories like this example be considered fragmentary myths?

○ R	○ U	○ Ap
⊙ An	⊙ E	○ C

26. Speedy delivery

Consider the use of mythological characters in advertising.
For example, florists who belong to Interflora use Mercury as their symbol or 'mascot'. Why is this choice appropriate? Can you find other examples of mythological characters being used in advertising?

⊙ R	⊙ U	○ Ap
○ An	○ E	○ C

27. Once upon a time

Find out what writers and artists refer to as 'the muse'. Research what Muses originally were and what they represented. Make a list which outlines all the details. (Also find out where the word 'memory' comes from).

⊙ R	⊙ U	⊙ Ap
○ An	○ E	○ C

28. Character collage

Select your favourite mythological character. Cut out magazine pictures, words, designs etc. to show the important traits this character has demonstrated. Arrange your selections to make a pleasing collage.

○ R	○ U	○ Ap
◉ An	○ E	◉ C

29. A definition

From what does the word 'mythology' originate? What was the true meaning?
How has the meaning changed over the years?

◉ R	◉ U	○ Ap
○ An	○ E	○ C

30. Dreamtime storytelling

Hold your own dreamtime gathering. Plan the celebration. Invite members of the group to share in the storytelling. You might like to retell real dreamtime stories or make up your own myths.

○ R	○ U	○ Ap
◉ An	○ E	◉ C

31. Aboriginal myths

Learn about the traditions of the Koori. What are some of the Koori myths? What rituals or celebrations do they have to share their dreamtime stories?

◉ R	◉ U	◉ Ap
○ An	○ E	○ C

32. Modern cultural figure

Create a mythological character to fit modern times. Write a brief character sketch to show personality traits, abilities and special powers.

○ R	○ U	○ Ap
◉ An	◉ E	◉ C

33. A family tree

Make a family tree for the Titans. Show their relationships to the other gods and goddesses in Greek mythology.

◉ R	◉ U	◉ Ap
○ An	○ E	○ C

34. Serious or entertaining

It is believed that myths were always told to convey serious meaning and never for amusement or entertainment. Do you agree with this idea? Give reasons to support your position.

○ R	○ U	○ Ap
⊙ An	⊙ E	○ C

35. Mythological journey

Which gods and goddesses appeared in Homer's epic *Ulysses*? Which ones did he offend? Which offered refuge and/or help? Make a list of those that appear in the story. Write a sentence or two about their role in Ulysses's search.

⊙ R	⊙ U	○ Ap
○ An	○ E	○ C

36. An even exchange

Using the character developed in activity 32, exchange your ideas with a classmate or partner. Each should incorporate the character developed by the other into an original modern myth after the stories are complete.

○ R	○ U	○ Ap
⊙ An	⊙ E	⊙ C

37. In the beginning

Greek and Roman mythology are well known because many statues and stories were left by these cultures. But older cultures and older myths than these exist. Research the most ancient civilisations you can find information on. Find out about their myths and legends. Compile a book to show your findings.

⊙ R	⊙ U	⊙ Ap
⊙ An	○ E	⊙ C

38. Myth of your own

Use the character you developed in activity 32. Create a myth in which this character is featured. Be sure the story is compatible with the features and traits you assigned to the character.

○ R   ○ U   ○ Ap
⊙ An   ○ E   ⊙ C

39. Artists' views

Many great works of art have been representations of the gods and goddesses in mythology. Study these art works. Resources in the library and a trip to an art gallery would be very helpful. Make a collection of pictures of such artwork.

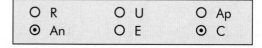

○ R   ○ U   ○ Ap
⊙ An   ○ E   ⊙ C

40. Name day

Some of our months are named after mythological characters. For example, Juno was a Roman deity used to name the month of June. See how many calendar months are named after mythological figures. Research the changes that were made to the calendar over the centuries. For example, the calendar was originally based on lunar cycles. Design and make a calendar that could show as much of this information as possible.

⊙ R   ⊙ U   ⊙ Ap
⊙ An   ○ E   ⊙ C

Fairytales, fables and legends

Fairytales, fables and legends

Activity	Remembering	Understanding	Applying	Analysing	Evaluating	Creating
1				x	x	
2				x	x	x
3	x	x	x			
4				x	x	x
5				x	x	
6		x	x	x		
7	x	x	x			
8	x	x		x	x	
9	x			x		
10		x	x	x		
11	x	x	x			
12				x		x
13	x	x	x			
14				x		x
15				x	x	x
16				x		x
17	x	x	x			
18		x		x	x	x
19				x	x	x
20	x					

Fairytales, fables and legends

Activity	Remembering	Understanding	Applying	Analysing	Evaluating	Creating
21		x		x		
22				x		x
23		x		x		x
24		x		x		
25				x	x	x
26		x				x
27		x		x	x	
28			x	x	x	x
29	x	x		x		
30		x				x
31	x	x		x	x	
32				x		
33			x	x		x
34		x		x	x	
35				x		x
36	x	x				
37				x	x	x
38	x	x		x		x
39	x	x	x	x	x	
40	x	x		x	x	

1. It's a wonder

Lewis Carroll is a modern writer of fairytales. Compare his *Alice in Wonderland* with fairytales by Andersen and the Grimms. Why might his book be classified as a fairytale?

O R	O U	O Ap
◉ An	◉ E	O C

2. Modern tales

Write a fairytale concerning modern problems. You may want your main character to face a crisis or problem related to energy.

O R	O U	O Ap
◉ An	◉ E	◉ C

3. The triad

In most fairytales things happen in threes. Find examples in several fairytales.

◉ R	◉ U	◉ Ap
O An	O E	O C

4. Frog or prince?

Why is the frog chosen to be the ugly character in so many tales? Would you make a change to this tradition? What change would you make and why?

O R	O U	O Ap
◉ An	◉ E	◉ C

5. The most awful

Of all the fairytales you have read, who was the meanest villain or scariest character? Why do you think so?

O R	O U	O Ap
◉ An	◉ E	O C

6. It's in the news

Write a newspaper account of the events in a well known fairytale. For example, you might choose to report on the ball attended by Cinderella. Use correct news journalism style.

O R	◉ U	◉ Ap
◉ An	O E	O C

7. Worldly tales

Fairytales come from all over the world. Classify tales you read according to the country of their origin. Locate these countries on a map. Make flags to note famous tales from different countries. How are they alike? How are they different?

◉ R	◉ U	◉ Ap
○ An	○ E	○ C

8. Famous beginnings

Fairytales are short stories of enchantment. The story usually starts out 'Once upon a time', or 'Long, long ago ...' Read a variety of fairytales. Identify the characters. What is the problem? What helps bring about a resolution? How does the story end? What is to be learned?

◉ R	◉ U	○ Ap
◉ An	◉ E	○ C

9. Lucky leprechauns

Leprechauns are fairy creatures popular in Irish culture. Describe a leprechaun. Investigate the beliefs of the Irish related to this elf character. What holiday do we celebrate that is taken from this culture? Research the significance of celebrating this custom.

◉ R	○ U	○ Ap
◉ An	○ E	○ C

10. Then and now

The early tales of Giovanni Straparola, Charles Perrault and Frances Browne are well known. Later come the writings of George MacDonald, Oscar Wilde and James Thurber. Compare and contrast the writings of these periods.

○ R	◉ U	◉ Ap
◉ An	○ E	○ C

11. Common beginnings

Fairytales

How do fairytales begin? List the introductions you find in those you read. What do the introductions have in common?

⊙ R	⊙ U	⊙ Ap
○ An	○ E	○ C

12. A mixed up story

Fairytales

Take five of your favourite fairytale characters. Mix them up in one story. You might want to make a cartoon or write a short play to illustrate or dramatise your mixed up tale.

○ R	○ U	○ Ap
⊙ An	○ E	⊙ C

13. Real life fairy land

Fairytales

Walt Disney has developed movies and park sections around fairytale characters. Read about Walt Disney's life. Write a factual report about him.

⊙ R	⊙ U	⊙ Ap
○ An	○ E	○ C

14. Send a card

Fairytales

Create a birthday party for one of your characters. Design a card for them. You might also want to write a song.

○ R	○ U	○ Ap
⊙ An	○ E	⊙ C

15. Plan a party

Fairytales

If you were planning a birthday party for a fairytale character, which five guests would you invite? Where in fairy land would you go? What would you serve?

○ R	○ U	○ Ap
⊙ An	⊙ E	⊙ C

16. How does your garden grow?

Fairytales

Design a new garden for Mary, Mary, Quite Contrary. What could she grow? Illustrate your garden.

○ R	○ U	○ Ap
⊙ An	○ E	⊙ C

17. Birthday celebration

The year 1978 was Mickey Mouse's fiftieth birthday. Try to find out how old these characters are: Cinderella, Red Riding Hood, Snugglepot, Blinky Bill, Rumpelstiltskin, Sleeping Beauty, Goldilocks, The Three Pigs, Hansel and Gretel, Mother Goose and Rapunzel. List their birthdates and ages.

⊙ R ⊙ U ⊙ Ap
○ An ○ E ○ C

18. Literary violence

Have you ever considered fairytales as being violent? Many people do. Think about and analyse ten fairytales. Give examples of violence for each of these. You could work as a group. Collect your data. Record your findings. Take a vote. Which fairytale is considered: 1. The most violent? 2. The least violent? Give your reasons.

○ R ⊙ U ○ Ap
⊙ An ⊙ E ⊙ C

19. Fairytale ecology

Thinking about ecology in our country – our throw-away culture. For example what 'throw aways' might the Good Fairy use to make Cinderella's coach and footmen? Explain what she might use. What could Cinderella's modern coach look like?

○ R ○ U ○ Ap
⊙ An ⊙ E ⊙ C

20. Meet Mr Aesop

Fables are short, fanciful stories used to explain a belief and contain a moral or value statement. Usually the characters are animals who behave and talk like humans. Aesop is probably the best known writer of fables. Research his life. Who was he? What was his background? What circumstances or conditions might have compelled him to write fables?

⊙ R ○ U ○ Ap
○ An ○ E ○ C

21. Fable comparisons

Fairytales

Read a wide variety of fables. How are they alike? How do they differ? Can you find any fables other than those by Aesop?

O R	⊙ U	O Ap
⊙ An	O E	O C

22. And then he said, '_____'.

Fairytales

Have fun! Make up some silly quotes from fairytale characters. Example: 'Nursery rhymes always crack me up', said Humpty Dumpty.

O R	O U	O Ap
⊙ An	O E	⊙ C

23. Morals and values

Fairytales

A moral statement or conclusion is made at or near the end of each fable. Locate these morals in the fables you read. Discuss how they are related to our modern standards or values.

O R	⊙ U	O Ap
⊙ An	O E	⊙ C

24. Lasting lines

Fairytales

Some expressions that we use have evolved from fables. An example is 'a wolf in sheep's clothing'. Explain the meaning of this phrase. Select other phrases that originated in fables. Give the meanings.

O R	⊙ U	O Ap
⊙ An	O E	O C

25. Parable of fable?

Fairytales

A parable is a short story which teaches a lesson. How is a parable like a fable? How are they different? Write a parable to teach a lesson about some conflict in your school, home or community.

O R	O U	O Ap
⊙ An	⊙ E	⊙ C

26. Modern fable

Fairytales

George Orwell's book *Animal Farm* might be considered a modern fable. Explain why you think this is true.

O R	⊙ U	O Ap
⊙ An	⊙ E	O C

27. Animal characters

Medieval tales and fables contain many animal characters. These animals are used to represent humans. For example, a pig in a story may represent a greedy person. Identify other animals in fables. Make a chart to show their characteristics.
How do these characteristics relate to the animals?

O R	⊙ U	O Ap
⊙ An	O E	O C

28. Animal traits

Animals are used in fables to demonstrate human characteristics. What animal character might be used to represent you? Why? Make animal associations for your friends or family members. Give reasons for choosing as you do.

O R	O U	⊙ Ap
⊙ An	⊙ E	⊙ C

29. Goblin market

Christina Rossetti wrote many poems and short stories about children in the 1800s. See if you can find a copy of the poem 'Goblin Market' or her collection of short stories *Speaking Likenesses*. As you read her poems and stories try to work out what the characters represent.

⊙ R	⊙ U	O Ap
⊙ An	O E	O C

30. Class collections

What is a proverb? Give examples of proverbs from fables you have read. Write proverbs of your own. You might interview your grandmother or grandfather to get 'sayings' from long ago. Make a class collection.

O R	⊙ U	O Ap
O An	O E	⊙ C

31. Character traits

List and compare fairytales which feature stepmothers as villainous characters. Why do you think they were portrayed this way?

- ⊙ R
- ⊙ An
- ⊙ U
- ⊙ E
- ○ Ap
- ○ C

32. Legendary characters

Australian legendary characters include Ned Kelly, Caroline Chisholm and Bennelong. What aspects of Australian history do you find in these legends?

- ○ R
- ⊙ An
- ○ U
- ○ E
- ○ Ap
- ○ C

33. Modern legends – modern events

Write a legend about some important event or person in your lifetime. Perhaps you will want to choose a natural event such as 'Ash Wednesday' as a starting point.

- ○ R
- ⊙ An
- ○ U
- ○ E
- ⊙ Ap
- ⊙ C

34. Who, what and when?

Legend of Sleepy Hollow by Washington Irving is an interesting story. Read it. Identify the elements: setting, protagonist, antagonist, plot, climax and resolution.

- ○ R
- ⊙ An
- ⊙ U
- ⊙ E
- ○ Ap
- ○ C

35. Sing a story

Compose and write lyrics for an original ballad. You might want to take an existing legend and set it to music.

- ○ R
- ⊙ An
- ○ U
- ○ E
- ○ Ap
- ⊙ C

36. Famous tellers of tales

Hans Christian Anderson and the Brothers Grimm are two of the best known writers of fairytales. Investigate their lives. Choose one or more and develop a biography.

- ⊙ R
- ○ An
- ⊙ U
- ○ E
- ○ Ap
- ○ C

37. 'Dear …'

What makes a person outstanding? What makes a character worth reading about? Choose a person in your life who has been or is an inspiration to you. Write a 'thank you' letter to this person expressing your feelings.

○ R	○ U	○ Ap
⊙ An	⊙ E	⊙ C

38. Tall tales

Legends are usually intertwined with tall tales (exaggerations). Many of these are from the pioneering days. Read about the early settlement of Australia. Use the tall tale technique to write a tall tale of historical fiction which incorporates both historical fact and exaggerates the character. Illustrate your story.

⊙ R	⊙ U	○ Ap
⊙ An	○ E	⊙ C

39. Pass it on

Legends are improbable, fanciful stories handed down by word of mouth. The story is usually interwoven with the history and people of a nation. The word legend implies a story to be read aloud. Choose a legend you enjoy. Read it aloud to the class using as much expression as possible.

⊙ R	⊙ U	⊙ Ap
⊙ An	⊙ E	○ C

40. Musical tales

Ballads are an integral part of Australian folk music. Identify and listen to several ballads. Do they have common characteristics? Do they qualify as legends? How? Give evidence to support your answers.

⊙ R	⊙ U	○ Ap
⊙ An	⊙ E	○ C

The supernatural

The supernatural

Activity	Remembering	Understanding	Applying	Analysing	Evaluating	Creating
1	x	x				
2	x	x	x			
3	x	x	x			
4				x	x	x
5				x	x	
6	x	x	x	x		x
7		x		x	x	x
8			x	x		x
9	x	x		x	x	
10	x	x		x		
11				x	x	x
12				x	x	x
13			x	x	x	x
14	x	x	x	x		
15	x	x	x	x		x
16	x	x		x	x	x

The supernatural

Activity	Remembering	Understanding	Applying	Analysing	Evaluating	Creating
17				x	x	x
18				x	x	x
19				x		x
20	x	x				
21	x	x				
22	x	x	x			
23	x	x				
24	x	x	x	x		x
25				x	x	x
26			x	x		x
27			x	x	x	x
28	x	x	x			
29	x	x	x			
30	x	x				
31	x	x	x			
32	x		x	x	x	x

1. Supernatural?

What is meant by 'the supernatural'? Prepare a list or chart to show ideas, words or characters associated with the supernatural.

⊙ R	⊙ U	○ Ap
○ An	○ E	○ C

2. Do you have E.S.P?

A great deal has been written about E.S.P. What is it? Read journal or magazine articles related to E.S.P. What are the major points being made about E.S.P?

⊙ R	⊙ U	⊙ Ap
○ An	○ E	○ C

3. Social structures

Research the history of witches in the Middle Ages. What are the characteristics of witches? Define a witch. What happened to witches during this time? Write a report on your findings.

⊙ R	⊙ U	⊙ Ap
○ An	○ E	○ C

4. Three wishes

If you could possess supernatural powers, which three would you desire? How would you use these powers to make our world a better place?

○ R	○ U	○ Ap
⊙ An	⊙ E	⊙ C

5. Favourite colour

Auras are supernatural phenomena. Find out what they are. If you had an aura, what colours would you prefer for different emotions, moods and feelings?

○ R	○ U	○ Ap
⊙ An	⊙ E	○ C

6. Circles of stone

Stonehenge has long been a mystery to people all over the world. Research the history of Stonehenge and record as many interesting facts as you can. Make a model of Stonehenge.

⊙ R	⊙ U	⊙ Ap
⊙ An	○ E	⊙ C

7. Super mystery solver

E.S.P or clairvoyance claims to be a help in solving mysteries all over the world. Read articles relating to these experiences. Report to your class. Conduct a survey. How many people, after listening to your report, accept this as a fact? How many require more information? Make a list of responses.

O R	⊙ U	O Ap
⊙ An	⊙ E	⊙ C

8. Let's pretend!

Just for fun, plan a seance in your classroom to give an example of how they work. Be sure to have all necessary background reading completed before the seance takes place.

Please note: Parent and teacher permission should be sought before this activity is conducted.

O R	O U	⊙ Ap
⊙ An	O E	⊙ C

9. Who's under the table?

Seances are sometimes conducted as a game at social gatherings. They are also conducted by people who claim to have special powers to contact the dead. Read about seances. Write about your reaction to these occurrences after reading and comparing related articles.

⊙ R	⊙ U	O Ap
⊙ An	⊙ E	O C

10. Wonderful wizard

In history, certain people were thought to have supernatural powers. Many of these people have been chosen as characters in the development of a story. Some characters might be wizards, witches, warlocks, sorcerers. Summarise the plot of a book or a story with specific examples of the characters' mystical abilities.

⊙ R	⊙ U	O Ap
⊙ An	O E	O C

11. Whooo are you?

If seances actually work, who would you like to communicate with from among the dead? What kinds of questions would you ask this person? What observations might this person make about life today?

○ R	○ U	○ Ap
⊙ An	⊙ E	⊙ C

12. Do you see what I see?

There are people who claim to have had visions. Sometimes they are religious, others are not. Religious visionaries have been persecuted, even executed. Can you give examples of these visionaries and their visions? What happened to them? Ask your librarian or media centre people to help with resources. Check several sources. What is your personal reaction to this information?

○ R	○ U	○ Ap
⊙ An	⊙ E	⊙ C

13. Experiment!

Conduct your own E.S.P experiment. Choose four cards each containing a different shape: circle, square, rectangle, triangle. Choosing two people, have one be the sender of messages concerning the shape; the other, the receiver. Decide upon a designated number of times to try their E.S.P. (You might want to find information on probabilities and averaging scores for these sorts of tests). Record your results in graph form. Do this with various pairs. What conclusions can you make from your data?

○ R	○ U	⊙ Ap
⊙ An	⊙ E	⊙ C

14. Fiery discs

What do you presently know about UFOs? Make a list of questions you would like answered about UFOs. Write a business letter to the Bureau of Meteorology or an astronomers association requesting answers to your questions.

⊙ R ⊙ U ⊙ Ap
⊙ An ○ E ○ C

15. Cults – cultures – subcultures

Research the different systems of religions in England from ancient times to the present day. Make a timeline to show when these beliefs were popular and include details about why people's beliefs have changed over the years.

⊙ R ⊙ U ⊙ Ap
⊙ An ○ E ⊙ C

16. Crystal ball illusions

Fortune tellers and their crystal balls are often at carnivals and resort locations. Pretend to be a fortune teller. Plan 'fortunes' for your class. Try to come up with realistic predictions. Find out why a crystal is used for 'gazing into'.

⊙ R ⊙ U ○ Ap
⊙ An ⊙ E ⊙ C

17. Future revelations

If a crystal ball could see into your future, what would you hope it would show? You might want to use a life-size cut-out of yourself and show your 'future' self. Include other relevant facts such as family, hobbies, interests and strengths.

○ R ○ U ○ Ap
⊙ An ⊙ E ⊙ C

18. Supernatural characters

After reading about supernatural characters, develop, characterise and illustrate your image for the Wise Witch, Wonderful Wizard, Sensational Sorcerer etc. Think about their needs to do their job.

O R   O U   O Ap
⊙ An   ⊙ E   ⊙ C

19. No clocks needed

What changes would occur if, in fact, time stood still?
Draw the imagined outcome in comic strip style.

O R   O U   O Ap
⊙ An   O E   ⊙ C

20. Second time 'round

Reincarnation is a belief of certain religions. How is reincarnation related to the Hindu religion? What other religions hold this belief?.

⊙ R   ⊙ U   O Ap
O An   O E   O C

21. Light power

Laser beams and laser powers were at one time used in comic strips and films to show characters with supernatural powers. Find out the many uses for the laser in science today.

⊙ R   ⊙ U   O Ap
O An   O E   O C

22. What is it?

Uri Geller has written a book dealing with psychokenesis. Find the meaning of this term. Locate information related to this field. Give an explanation to your group.

⊙ R   ⊙ U   ⊙ Ap
O An   O E   O C

23. Who do voodoo?

In America, Africa and Haiti, voodoo has long been practised. Explain voodoo and its uses by various cultures.

⊙ R   ⊙ U   O Ap
O An   O E   O C

24. Ace of hearts

There are various card games and tricks which supposedly tell one's future. Locate, investigate and try your hand at 'good fortune' telling. Research the history of playing cards. Design your own 52 card deck.

⊙ R   ⊙ U   ⊙ Ap
⊙ An   ○ E   ⊙ C

25. My life as a ...

If you were to be reincarnated, what person, animal or being would you choose as your next life form? Give your reasons for your choice. What would you want from your next life? You might want to have a picture showing examples of your desired reincarnations.

○ R   ○ U   ○ Ap
⊙ An   ⊙ E   ⊙ C

26. Number, please?

In the realm of the supernatural, anything can happen. Think about a day when all the numbers disappear. How would this change your life?
Write a journal page giving your step by step activities for a day without numbers.

○ R   ○ U   ⊙ Ap
⊙ An   ○ E   ⊙ C

27. Have a drink

Pretend you are a scientist developing a magic potion which would give supernatural powers to anyone who drinks it. Use your imagination to develop this delightful drink. Tell why your ingredients are used and what purpose they serve. Each ingredient should give special powers. For example: carrot juice for x-ray eyes.

○ R   ○ U   ⊙ Ap
⊙ An   ⊙ E   ⊙ C

28. Energy and matter

Scientists have recently been able to identify and quantify phenomena that have not been generally understood up until now. Find out about as many of these discoveries as you can and make a list. (Scientific magazines will be an easy source of information).

⊙ R	⊙ U	⊙ Ap
O An	O E	O C

29. Supernatural science

Duke University is the leading centre in the United States for the study of science, particularly parapsychology. What is this science? Write to Duke University to get information about their department and course offerings. Are similar courses offered in Australian universities?

⊙ R	⊙ U	⊙ Ap
O An	O E	O C

30. Camera magic

The Soviet Union developed a special form of photography which has been used to photograph auras. What is this method called? How is it special? How is it being used in the medical profession for diagnosis?

⊙ R	⊙ U	O Ap
O An	O E	O C

31. Life forces

Find information on the many forms of energy that sustain the human mind and body. Draw a diagram to show how these forces enable us to think and move.

⊙ R	⊙ U	⊙ Ap
O An	O E	O C

32. Magical pyramid

Pyramid power is being researched in a laboratory in California to determine its energy and special forces – if any. Various books and articles are available concerning this subject. Read about it. Construct your own pyramid and carry out your own investigation. You might want to attempt plant growth or food preservation. Be sure to develop a hypothesis and scientifically record data regarding heat, light, observations etc. Complete the project by writing your conclusions. You may also want to include some recommendations.

| ⊙ R | ○ U | ⊙ Ap |
| ⊙ An | ⊙ E | ⊙ C |

Adventure

Adventure

Activity	Remebering	Understanding	Applying	Analysing	Evaluating	Creating
1	x	x				
2					x	x
3	x	x	x			
4		x	x	x	x	x
5				x		x
6				x	x	x
7	x	x	x			
8	x	x				
9	x	x		x		x
10	x	x		x		x
11	x	x	x			
12	x	x	x			
13		x	x			
14				x		x
15	x	x	x			
16		x		x	x	x
17				x	x	x
18		x		x	x	x
19				x	x	
20				x	x	x

Adventure

Activity	Remebering	Understanding	Applying	Analysing	Evaluating	Creating
21				x	x	x
22		x		x		x
23		x				
24				x	x	x
25		x	x			
26				x	x	x
27						x
28				x		x
29						x
30				x	x	
31		x	x		x	
32				x	x	
33			x	x		x
34		x				
35				x	x	x
36				x	x	x
37					x	x
38	x	x	x			
39	x	x		x		x
40				x	x	

1. Book records

Write a short summary of each adventure story you read. Give the story title, the book, author and page numbers.
Then summarise the story in a few sentences.

⊙ R   ⊙ U   ○ Ap
○ An   ○ E   ○ C

2. Personal tales

Sometimes we have unexpected adventures in our lives. Think of a time when you had an adventure. Write a short account of your experiences.

○ R   ○ U   ○ Ap
○ An   ⊙ E   ⊙ C

3. It's true

Many adventure stories are true. You have probably read about people who have been stranded in the wilderness and survived, or people who have saved others in danger. Select one of these true adventure stories. Tell the story in your own words.

⊙ R   ⊙ U   ⊙ Ap
○ An   ○ E   ○ C

4. Today's tales

Can you think of some modern day adventures? Can you make a past to present timeline to show adventures of people who dared to explore the unknown?

○ R   ⊙ U   ⊙ Ap
⊙ An   ⊙ E   ⊙ C

5. Write your own

Using the *Adventures of Pinocchio* as a model, write a story to teach others a lesson of value.

○ R   ○ U   ○ Ap
⊙ An   ○ E   ⊙ C

6. A super trip

Suppose you could choose one super adventure trip. Where would you go? What would happen on your trip? Can you tell your story with pictures? Make an adventure style picture book and show your travels.

○ R   ○ U   ○ Ap
⊙ An   ⊙ E   ⊙ C

7. The word

Adventure is a word we use often and in different ways. Write in your own words what you think the word 'adventure' means. Now look in at least two dictionaries. Read their definitions. Compare them with yours. Use this information to help you write a short paragraph to show what the word 'adventure' means.

⊙ R	⊙ U	⊙ Ap
O An	O E	O C

8. Nature and adventures

Sometimes nature creates adventures for us. Earthquakes, storms, volcanoes and other natural events may cause people to have unexpected adventures. Read at least one story about a natural disaster and the adventures related to it. Summarise your reading by telling what adventures or experiences were caused by the natural event.

⊙ R	⊙ U	O Ap
O An	O E	O C

9. In suspense

Suspense is another word often related to adventure stories. In many cases the character or characters in the adventure story have experiences that keep the reader in suspense. Select two or three stories with an element of suspense. When did you as the reader feel anxious or suspenseful? How did the author make you feel this way? Give examples. Write your own suspenseful segment.

⊙ R	⊙ U	O Ap
⊙ An	O E	⊙ C

10. Picture reports

Record the books you used in this study by illustrating one or more of the adventures. Below your pictures write the adventures and a caption. The picture or pictures should reflect the highlights of the adventure. Choose carefully.

⊙ R	⊙ U	O Ap
⊙ An	O E	⊙ C

11. Early adventures

Sometimes adventures are exciting because they explore the unknown. Consider some of these early explorers:

| Marco Polo | Burke and Wills | Captain Cook |
| Columbus | Magellan | Strzelecki |

Continued in activity 12.

⊙ R   ⊙ U   ⊙ Ap
○ An   ○ E   ○ C

12. Early adventures (cont. from activity 11)

Read something about their explorations. Would you say they lead adventurous lives? Give reasons. What did each accomplish that was the result of an adventure? Use the chart to help you.

Explorer	Adventure	Outcome

⊙ R   ⊙ U   ⊙ Ap
○ An   ○ E   ○ C

13. Personal danger

Have you ever been in danger or perhaps injured while alone? Describe your feelings. How did your feelings affect your behaviour? What was the outcome?

○ R   ⊙ U   ⊙ Ap
○ An   ○ E   ○ C

14. Reverse it

Following the same process as in activity 28, start with an adventure story. You write the news article that might report it. Remember, only report the facts.

○ R   ○ U   ○ Ap
⊙ An   ○ E   ⊙ C

15. The classics

Some of the classic adventure stories are about Robin Hood, Tom Sawyer, Gulliver, Odysseus and Don Quixote. Select one of these classics to read. In each will be a variety of adventures. List the adventures the main character has. What was the outcome of each? Make a chart to help you.

⊙ R   ⊙ U   ⊙ Ap
○ An   ○ E   ○ C

16. Pioneer people

What adventures might the early settlers have had during the 1700s and 1800s? Consider what our country was like. Select an episode and describe the adventures of a settler family. Perhaps you could write a play and produce it.

○ R   ⊙ U   ○ Ap
⊙ An   ⊙ E   ⊙ C

17. Talking objects

If objects could talk they would be able to share all kinds of adventures. Remember Disney's movie *The Love Bug* and all the adventures the little VW had? Choose an inanimate object. Follow it around for a while in your mind. Write a story from the object's point of view. Some examples might be: The Adventures of Rosie Raindrop (or Susie Snowflake); A Pencil's Perils; A House Tells All.

○ R   ○ U   ○ Ap
⊙ An   ⊙ E   ⊙ C

18. Animal stories

Sometimes animals have adventures. Cats get caught in trees, dogs find their way home over long distances, horses win races. Choose your favourite animal. Make an animal adventure story. The animal is your main character. What adventures does the animal have?

○ R   ⊙ U   ○ Ap
⊙ An   ⊙ E   ⊙ C

19. Pinocchio's adventures

In the *Adventures of Pinocchio*, telling lies caused much trouble for one wooden boy. This story was written to teach us a lesson. Explain the moral or lesson in this story. How did the adventures help to develop the story? Explain.

O R   O U   O Ap
⊙ An   ⊙ E   O C

20. Forever and always

In the book *Tuck Everlasting* the character comes upon a spring and drinks from it. The water stops the ageing process. Consider the effects of drinking from a fountain of youth. Tell about your experiences as those around you age and you do not. What are the advantages and disadvantages? Would you drink from it again if you could turn back time?

O R   O U   O Ap
⊙ An   ⊙ E   ⊙ C

21. Stranded!

Pretend that you and a friend have wandered away from the others. It is night time. You find yourself in a wooded area as it grows dark. You try and try to find your way back to the group, but have no luck. You are hopelessly lost. It is very dark and getting cold. What do you do?

O R   O U   O Ap
⊙ An   ⊙ E   ⊙ C

22. Thar she blows!

When Mt St Helens erupted, much property was destroyed, but few lives were lost. This is not always the case. Suppose that all of a sudden a volcano erupted near your home. Describe what is going on. Make your readers feel they are there.

O R   ⊙ U   O Ap
⊙ An   O E   ⊙ C

23. Opposite sides

Sometimes a story or incident can be seen from several points of view. Think of a time when you might have been in a situation that was scary to you. When you found out the truth, it was kind of funny. Describe the incident.

O R	⊙ U	O Ap
O An	O E	O C

24. Picture this

Using old magazines, cut out pictures that show a possible setting for an adventure story. Mount them on cardboard. On the back, write a short story beginning. Exchange pictures with a classmate. Finish each other's story.

O R	O U	O Ap
⊙ An	⊙ E	⊙ C

25. Real-life adventure

Firefighters, police officers, hospital workers and others find themselves in adventure packed situations as part of normal work activities. Interview one or more of these people to find out how they deal with real life adventure. How does it affect their behaviour?

O R	⊙ U	⊙ Ap
O An	O E	O C

26. Fairytale adventures

Using the traditional fairytales, look at the possibilities for adventure stories. Suppose that Red Riding Hood or Goldilocks were reporting the experiences first hand. What would be different? Choose one fairytale and rewrite it as an adventure.

O R	O U	O Ap
⊙ An	⊙ E	⊙ C

27. The find

Have you ever wanted to find a hidden treasure? Use your imagination to draw a super treasure map. Don't tell what the treasure is. Exchange your map with someone else. Write the story for the treasure you 'find'.

○ R	○ U	○ Ap
○ An	○ E	⊙ C

28. It's news

Scan the newspaper. Find a news account of some action. For example, you may read about a rock slide in a mountain area. Read the news story carefully. Now using that information, and your imagination, change it to an adventure story.

○ R	○ U	○ Ap
⊙ An	○ E	⊙ C

29. Diary of experiences

You have set sail in a small boat off the coast of a resort. Waters are supposed to be safe and the last weather report predicted clear skies and smooth sailing. A sudden storm springs up. You are washed out to sea. Keep a diary telling of your experiences.

○ R	○ U	○ Ap
○ An	○ E	⊙ C

30. Adventurous melodies

Some music builds a mood of adventure. Watch adventure shows on TV. Listen to the background music. How does the music help to build the feeling of adventure? Tape a collection of adventure building musical selections. Ask others to tell what action might be going on.

○ R	○ U	○ Ap
⊙ An	⊙ E	○ C

31. Watch your step!

Shadows, creaking floorboards and sudden noises help to build tension in films and television shows. Make a list of sounds and images that are often used to make adventures more dramatic. Why do these have such an effect on the audience?

O R	⊙ U	⊙ Ap
O An	⊙ E	O C

32. Modern pirates

Pirates of old had hair-raising adventures on the high seas. Today's pirates are 'breaking into' computers and 'pirating' programs. How are these pirates like those of days gone by? Is their pirating an adventure? Is it okay to be a video pirate or computer pirate?

O R	O U	O Ap
⊙ An	⊙ E	O C

33. Tall tales

A tall tale is an adventure or a series of adventures written with exaggeration. Take a particular adventure you have had or wish you had experienced. What things about the adventure could you exaggerate? Which of your characteristics could you exaggerate? Tell your tall tale to a younger group of students after you have practised it.

O R	O U	⊙ Ap
⊙ An	O E	⊙ C

34. It's a challenge

Has anyone ever dared you to do something you thought was dangerous? What happened? Did you do it? How did you handle the dare? Write an adventurous, suspensful account of the dare you completed.

O R	⊙ U	O Ap
O An	O E	O C

35. Pet tales

If you have a pet who is outdoors a great deal, your pet may have adventures of its own. Pretend that your pet can talk. Write a story in which the pet is telling you about its adventure. Make your story possible.

| O R | O U | O Ap |
| ⊙ An | ⊙ E | ⊙ C |

36. Survival

You and a friend have wandered away from home and met with an accident. It is almost dark and getting cold. There is no way you can get back home. What do you do? Tell what has happened and what action you will take.

| O R | O U | O Ap |
| ⊙ An | ⊙ E | ⊙ C |

37. And what happened then?

Read a newspaper. Identify a happening that created an adventurous situation. It might be a storm, earthquake etc. Develop a news story to tell about the adventure. Remember in a news story you must keep your facts straight; however, you can use descriptive words to paint a picture.

| O R | O U | O Ap |
| O An | ⊙ E | ⊙ C |

38. True adventure

Make a list of people in history who have had true life adventures. See how many adventurers you can name. You may wish to categorise them as to their adventure. Here are some to get you started: Tony Bullimore, Neil Armstrong, Wilbur and Orville Wright, Jane Goodall.

| ⊙ R | ⊙ U | ⊙ Ap |
| O An | O E | O C |

39. Problems! Problems!

Adventure stories usually put the main character in a situation where there is a problem to solve. Read several adventure stories. Make a chart to show this story element.

Story	Character	Problem

⊙ R	⊙ U	○ Ap
⊙ An	○ E	⊙ C

40. Adventure and the unknown

Adventure usually comes from not understanding the circumstances or not having all the information. For example, think of the landing of the First Fleet as a routine historical report. If you had been a convict, it would have been an extraordinary experience. Choose a historical character. Rewrite the event in first person to show the adventurous details.

○ R	○ U	○ Ap
⊙ An	○ E	⊙ C

Dreams

Dreams

Activity	Remembering	Understanding	Applying	Analysing	Evaluating	Creating
1	x	x		x		x
2						x
3		x		x	x	x
4				x		x
5				x		x
6				x	x	x
7	x	x				
8	x	x				
9	x	x				
10		x		x		
11	x	x				
12				x	x	
13		x		x		x
14				x	x	
15				x	x	
16	x	x		x		
17	x	x				x
18	x	x		x	x	x
19	x	x		x		
20	x	x				

Dreams

Activity	Remembering	Understanding	Applying	Analysing	Evaluating	Creating
21	x	x				
22		x			x	x
23		x		x	x	x
24	x	x			x	
25				x	x	
26		x		x		x
27	x	x				
28		x		x	x	
29				x	x	x
30				x	x	
31		x	x	x	x	
32		x		x	x	x
33		x	x	x		
34		x	x	x		
35		x				x
36				x	x	
37				x	x	x
38	x	x		x	x	
39		x		x	x	
40				x	x	x

1. Dream dancer

The activity title is the name of a horse in the book by Evelyn Bolton. Read the book to find out why this horse is called Dream Dancer. Then take it a step further. Create an animal character with a dream reference in the name. Describe and illustrate your character.

⊙ R	⊙ U	O Ap
⊙ An	O E	⊙ C

2. Dream tree

Use an old branch or a paper cut-out tree. Make a noticeboard or display area called 'The Dream Tree'. Ask classmates to pin dreams or goals to the Dream Tree. Each dream could be written on a leaf shape. Others will enjoy sharing dreams. These should be 'dreams' that one has for oneself.

O R	O U	O Ap
O An	O E	⊙ C

3. Someday

Charlotte Zolotow has written a beautiful book called *Someday*. The little girl thinks about how things are and how they might be – someday – when she grows up. For example, she wishes that someday her brother would introduce her by saying, 'This is my sister', instead of 'Here is the family creep!' Think about your someday wishes. Make a picture book as Ms Zolotow did.

O R	⊙ U	O Ap
⊙ An	⊙ E	⊙ C

4. Dream artists

Some artists and musicians including Mozart, Henry Tuseli and Francisco Goya claim to have received inspiration and direction through dreams. Can you take a dream you've had and create music or a picture that describes it?

O R	O U	O Ap
⊙ An	O E	⊙ C

5. Dream mysteries

The *Dream Hunter* by Elinor Lyon is a Scottish mystery story involving dreams. Think how a dream might be worked into a mystery. Perhaps the 'victim' would dream of impending danger or the 'sleuth' would dream of a solution. Write a mystery story in which a dream plays a role in the story.

O R	O U	O Ap
⊙ An	O E	⊙ C

6. Dreams and writing

In the story *Dreams of Victory* by Ellen Conford, Victory does not feel very confident. Then she has a dream in which her imagination gives her an idea for a great school composition. Do you have a dream that can be turned into a super story? Add details, but use the dream for a basis.

O R	O U	O Ap
⊙ An	⊙ E	⊙ C

7. Sleep stages

Scientists who study dreams and sleep patterns know that people in a state of sleep go through several different sleep stages. Investigate to find out about the four sleep stages. Describe each of the stages and give the characteristics of each.

⊙ R	⊙ U	O Ap
O An	O E	O C

8. Dream poet

Langston Hughes is a famous poet who has written numerous poems about dreams or being influenced by dreams. 'Dream Keeper' is one example. Find other Langston Hughes poems. Read and collect them. What dream influences do you see?

⊙ R	⊙ U	O Ap
O An	O E	O C

9. Dream symbols

Dream research seems to indicate that some items are symbolic and represent other things. For example, crossing a river is thought to mean a turning point or a challenge. See if you can find the symbolic meaning for these and then add others to the list.

- Kings and Queens
- A long journey
- Small animals

- A crab
- Bridge
- Flying

- A road or path
- House
- Water

⊙ R   ⊙ U   ○ Ap
○ An   ○ E   ○ C

10. Brainwave bonanza

Modern science allows dream researchers to use studies of brainwaves to help analyse the behaviours of the mind. The electroencephalograph is used. Find out about this instrument. What does it do? How does it work? How does it help us to know more about thinking? Who was responsible for this important discovery?

○ R   ⊙ U   ○ Ap
⊙ An   ○ E   ○ C

11. Psychic dreams

Many people claim to have had psychic dreams. What are psychic dreams? Some people who have had psychic dreams include Rudyard Kipling, Abraham Lincoln and Jean Dixon. These people are very diverse. Find out about each and identify ways that psychic dreams have influenced their lives.

⊙ R   ⊙ U   ○ Ap
○ An   ○ E   ○ C

12. Drugs and dreams

Some drugs such as chloropromazine and reserpine are used to suppress or reduce dreams or dream tendency. Why might such drugs be used? Can you think of advantages and disadvantages for use of these drugs? Under what circumstances would they be helpful or harmful?

○ R	○ U	○ Ap
⊙ An	⊙ E	○ C

13. Dream solutions

Scientist Friedrich Kekulé is said to have worked for years on the molecular structure of benzene without success. One night he 'dreamed' the solution and was right. Have you ever had a dream that solved a problem for you? Tell about your experience.

○ R	⊙ U	○ Ap
⊙ An	○ E	⊙ C

14. Symbols and you

Refer to your findings in activity 9 to review universal dream symbols. Consider one or more dreams you have experienced. Have you had any of these symbols occur? Does the interpretation seem to apply? Explain your answer.

○ R	○ U	○ Ap
⊙ An	⊙ E	○ C

15. Predictive dreams

Many researchers believe you can 'program' your mind to experience dreams. Before you go to sleep, try this experiment by asking yourself questions about the future. Try this for several nights. Record your results in a journal. Check them as time allows.

○ R	○ U	○ Ap
⊙ An	⊙ E	○ C

16. Dream interpreter

Find out about the work of the Roman researcher Artemidorus. What was his work? How have his accomplishments influenced the current dream research?

⊙ R   ⊙ U   O Ap
⊙ An   O E   O C

17. Dream poems

Review poetry anthologies. Find and collect examples of ways different poets write about their dreams. Make a dream and poems scrapbook. Add some of your own.

⊙ R   ⊙ U   O Ap
O An   O E   ⊙ C

18. Mind altering

Some drugs induce hallucinations. Is this the same as dreaming? Explain. What are the dangers of using mind-altering drugs? Use research to support your position.

⊙ R   ⊙ U   O Ap
⊙ An   ⊙ E   ⊙ C

19. Dreamtime

Find out what part dreams play in Aboriginal culture. You may wish to examine the beliefs of one tribe or several so that you can compare tribal differences, if any.

⊙ R   ⊙ U   O Ap
⊙ An   O E   O C

20. Sleep disorder

There are numerous sleep disorder centres involved in sleep and dream research. Find out where the centre nearest you is located. Ask the centre what research is being done.

⊙ R   ⊙ U   O Ap
O An   O E   O C

21. REMs or NREMs

These letters are abbreviations used in connection with dream research. Explain what each means.

⊙ R   ⊙ U   O Ap
O An   O E   O C

22. Dream pictures

Raymond Briggs has authored a wordless book called *The Snowman*. Review the book. Is the boy dreaming? What evidence is there? How does the artist make you feel the dream quality? Use your artistic talent to make a picture book about one of your dreams. Share it with a younger child.

○ R	⊙ U	○ Ap
⊙ An	⊙ E	⊙ C

23. Nightmares

Children sometimes experience nightmares. What are the characteristics of a nightmare experience? Have you ever had a dream you would consider a nightmare? Describe it. How does it fit the nightmare model? Can you figure out what caused the nightmare?

○ R	⊙ U	○ Ap
⊙ An	⊙ E	⊙ C

24. Dream work

Have you ever had a dream in which you dreamed you worked so hard that when you awoke you felt tired? Describe it. Why do you think this dream might have occurred? What were the circumstances before and after the dream?

⊙ R	⊙ U	○ Ap
○ An	⊙ E	○ C

25. Dream practice

Jack Nicklaus, a famous golfer, claims that he 'practises' his golf in his dreams. Try to program your dreams for a two week period to 'practise' a particular skill. Do you see any actual improvement? Be specific. Would you endorse Nicklaus's belief in dream practice?

○ R	○ U	○ Ap
⊙ An	⊙ E	○ C

26. Frightening dreams

Sometimes we have terrifying dreams in different forms. Some of these might be nightmares, night terrors or anxiety dreams. Research each type. Make a chart to show the differences and similarities of each type.

O R	⊙ U	O Ap
⊙ An	O E	⊙ C

27. Telepathy research

Some work has been done with telepathy and E.S.P relating to dreams. Much of the work has been done by the Maimonides Medical Centre in America. Find out about the work being done there and report your findings.

⊙ R	⊙ U	O Ap
O An	O E	O C

28. Dream art

Famous artists claim to have had their works influenced by dreams. One of these is Francisco Goya. Another is Henry Tuseli in his work called *The Nightmare*. Gather examples of art related to dreams or as a result of dreams. What techniques do artists use to convey dream experiences? Which artist do you feel does the best job of representing dreams? Describe why?

O R	⊙ U	O Ap
⊙ An	⊙ E	O C

29. Under the bed

Many young children have dreams about animals or monsters that live under their beds. What was yours? Survey other members of your class to discover what was under the bed in their dreams. Report your results in graph form. What commonalities do you find? Why do you think you dream about animals under your bed?

O R	O U	O Ap
⊙ An	⊙ E	⊙ C

30. Dream writer

Samuel Taylor Coleridge claims that his famous poem 'Kubla Khan' came to him in a dream and that he only recorded it. Read the poem. What do you think? Could this have been received in a dream? Explain your response.

○ R	○ U	○ Ap
◉ An	◉ E	○ C

31. Dream diary

Keep a pad and pencil by your bed during this study. Each evening, program your mind to remember your dreams. When you get up each day, record what you remember about your dreams. Do you see any patterns emerging? Report what you find out about your own dreams.

○ R	◉ U	◉ Ap
◉ An	◉ E	○ C

32. Fantasy or reality?

Review your dream diary (from activity 31). Are your dreams mostly dealing with reality or fantasy? Classify your dreams under the two categories. What do you understand about the sort of dreams you are having?

○ R	◉ U	○ Ap
◉ An	◉ E	○ C

33. Colour or not?

Some people dream in colour. Others dream in black and white. Some of us dream in both together or at different times. Conduct a survey among your classmates to indicate the frequency of these dream types. Also, see if the dream patterns differ between boys and girls.

○ R	◉ U	○ Ap
◉ An	◉ E	◉ C

34. Common themes

Dream research indicates that many of us experience similar dreams. Below is a list of common dreams. Ask 20 people to indicate if they have had dreams in any category. Review your results. Does your sample population have common dreams?

- Walking through railway stations, bus terminals, airports and other crowded public places
- Riding in elevators
- Missing trains, planes and buses
- Growing larger or getting smaller
- Running fast without getting anywhere
- Falling through the air

- Flying through the air
- Running away from animals
- Losing teeth
- Snakes
- Being mugged

O R	⊙ U	⊙ Ap
⊙ An	O E	O C

35. Clairvoyance and dreams

Edgar Cayce, Kreskin, Eileen Garrett and Rosalind Heywood are just a few of the clairvoyants who claim to have received messages in a trance or dream state. What is clairvoyance? What is a trance? Do you believe that such people can actually 'see' the future? Base your opinion on the research you have done.

O R	⊙ U	O Ap
O An	O E	⊙ C

36. Pet dreams

Observe your pet as it sleeps. Watch muscle and eye movement carefully. From what you know about REMs and NREMs as they relate to dreams, would you say that your pet dreams? What evidence do you have?

O R	O U	O Ap
⊙ An	⊙ E	O C

37. Day or night

Are daydreams the same as our dreams at night? Explain the similarities and differences. Are both dreams? Explain your answer.

○ R	○ U	○ Ap
⊙ An	⊙ E	⊙ C

38. Right brain/Left brain

Current research is being done that indicates that each side of the brain 'thinks' in a different fashion. Research to find out what right brain and left brain thinking involves. How are they different? Which side of your brain is dominant? Note: There are tests to use!

⊙ R	⊙ U	○ Ap
⊙ An	⊙ E	○ C

39. Right or left dreams

Which side of your brain is probably involved in dreaming? Consider the functions you discovered in activity 38. With this in mind, what functions appear to be involved? Explain your answer.

○ R	⊙ U	○ Ap
⊙ An	⊙ E	○ C

40. Pet nightmares

If pets dream, does that mean they also have nightmares? What would be the typical nightmare of a pet dog, cat, fish or rabbit? Draw a picture of each pet's nightmare.

○ R	○ U	○ Ap
⊙ An	⊙ E	⊙ C

Superstition

Superstition

Activity	Remembering	Understanding	Applying	Analysing	Evaluating	Creating
1		x	x	x	x	
2		x		x	x	x
3	x	x	x			
4				x	x	x
5	x	x				
6		x		x	x	
7		x	x	x		
8				x		x
9				x	x	
10		x		x		x
11		x		x	x	x
12		x		x		x
13		x		x		x
14		x		x	x	
15		x	x	x	x	x
16				x	x	
17				x	x	x
18				x	x	x

Superstition

Activity	Remembering	Understanding	Applying	Analysing	Evaluating	Creating
19	x	x	x			
20	x	x	x	x		
21	x	x		x		x
22				x	x	x
23		x	x	x		
24		x	x			
25		x		x	x	
26	x	x	x	x		
27	x	x	x			x
28		x		x	x	x
29		x		x		x
30		x		x	x	x
31		x	x	x	x	
32	x	x		x	x	
33	x	x		x	x	
34	x	x	x		x	
35		x		x	x	x
36		x	x	x		x

1. Lucky colours

There are many rhymes and sayings that report luck or lack of it related to colour. Find some of these. Do you have a lucky colour? Does one colour seem to be best for you? Explain.

O R	⊙ U	⊙ Ap
⊙ An	⊙ E	O C

2. Birthstones

Birthstones are said to be lucky. Make a chart to show birthstones for each month. Turn the chart into a matching game. Have others try to match the month with the stone.

O R	⊙ U	O Ap
⊙ An	⊙ E	⊙ C

3. Four leaf clover

Find the traditional saying which explains the lucky powers of the four leaf clover. Draw a clover. Write the verse so that each line is written on a separate petal or leaf.

⊙ R	⊙ U	⊙ Ap
O An	O E	O C

4. Superstitious test

Make a list of at least ten superstitions. Test others to find out which they believe. Chart your results. Rate your participants as to their level of superstition.

O R	O U	O Ap
⊙ An	⊙ E	⊙ C

5. Pooh! Pooh!

A. A. Milne, creator of Winnie the Pooh, once said, 'Life must be tricky for the superstitious'. Explain what you believe he meant by this statement.

⊙ R	⊙ U	O Ap
O An	O E	O C

6. Does a dowser do?

What is a dowser? Can you explain the process a dowser goes through? What is the purpose? Does it work? Is this a scientific fact or not? What evidence do you have?

O R	⊙ U	O Ap
⊙ An	⊙ E	O C

7. Sports superstitions

There are many superstitions connected with various sports. Collect as many of these as you can and compile a booklet. Check it out with local teams. Do they follow any of these superstitions before a game? Explain your findings.

O R	⊙ U	⊙ Ap
⊙ An	O E	O C

8. Brides and luck

Brides often consider this rhyme when planning their wedding:
    Something old, something new
    something borrowed,
    something blue.
Survey the women who have been married in your family, neighbourhood and school. Did they follow this guide? Make a chart to show how many were affected by this superstition. Find out where this rhyme comes from and what it means.

O R	O U	O Ap
⊙ An	O E	⊙ C

9. 13th floor

So many people believe that the 13th floor of a hotel or building is unlucky that many buildings omit that number. Call hotels and high rises in your area to find out whether they have a 13th floor or not. Does not numbering the floor 13 change one's luck? Explain your answer.

O R	O U	O Ap
⊙ An	⊙ E	O C

10. Story fun

Wait Till the Moon Is Full is a story written by Margaret Wise Brown. Read the story. Around what superstition is the story based? Can you write a story for a children's picture book based on a superstition?

O R	⊙ U	O Ap
⊙ An	O E	⊙ C

11. Superstitions anthology

Cross Your Fingers, Spit in Your Hat is a collection of superstitions put together by Alvin Schwartz. Read the book. Make your own collection of favourite superstitions. What will you call it? What tales will be included? Illustrate it.

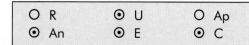

12. Creature curiosities

Many folktales and legends have been written about animals and the superstitions that surround them. In some countries, for example, when squirrels work extra hard to put nuts away for the winter, many people believe it is the sign of a harsh winter season. Find other animal related superstitions. Make an animal superstitions book.

13. Imaginary creatures

The imaginary creatures listed below all have something to do with luck – good or bad. Research each one. What luck influence is there? Make a book of these creatures. Include an illustration and several important details as well as how each creature is involved with luck.

- Banshee
- Brownie
- Demon
- Dwarf
- Elf
- Fairy
- Genie
- Ghost
- Ghoul
- Giant
- Gnome
- Goblin
- Gremlin
- Imp
- Leprechaun
- Little People
- Mermaid
- Merman
- Ogre
- Pixie
- Poltergeist
- Spirit
- Troll
- Vampire
- Werewolf
- Zombie

O R	⊙ U	O Ap
⊙ An	O E	⊙ C

14. Famous leaders

Some famous leaders believed in certain superstitions. For example, Napoleon and Hitler believed in the star of destiny. Churchill believed that Fridays were unlucky. Research to find how these beliefs affected their behaviours and decisions.
Add other famous leaders to your study.

O R	⊙ U	O Ap
⊙ An	⊙ E	O C

15. ABCs

There are superstitions that deal with subjects from A to Z. Research to find at least one superstitious belief from each letter of the alphabet. For example: If you pull on the wishbone (breast bone) of a chicken with a partner and it breaks, the person with the largest piece will have good luck. Categorise your choices. State the origin of the superstition. Illustrate. Share your book with others.

O R	⊙ U	⊙ Ap
⊙ An	⊙ E	⊙ C

16. Birth omen

Here is a popular birth omen rhyme. On which day were you born? Has your life been influenced by the omen or prediction? Explain.

Monday's child is fair of face,
Tuesday's child is full of grace,
Wednesday's child is loving and giving,
Thursday's child must work for a living,
Friday's child is full of woe,
Saturday's child has a journey to go,
But the child who is born on the Sabbath day
Is merry and happy and wise and gay.

O R	O U	O Ap
⊙ An	⊙ E	O C

17. Birthday candles

It is said to be good luck to blow out all the candles on your birthday cake with one breath. Find out the reasons for this belief. Have you ever made a wish and blown all the candles out? Did your wish come true? Write a story in which this happens.

| ○ R | ○ U | ○ Ap |
| ⊙ An | ⊙ E | ⊙ C |

18. Do you believe?

There are people who practise phrenology. Investigate this belief. These people believe that you can determine character by the shape of the head or by unusual features. Survey students and adults to find out if they believe in these phrenology concepts. Do you believe these are beliefs based in science or superstition? Explain your answer.

| ○ R | ○ U | ○ Ap |
| ⊙ An | ⊙ E | ⊙ C |

19. Curls, bobs, perms and pages

There are many beliefs about the cutting and disposing of hair. Many stories have also been told about the power attributed to long hair. Find out from friends, family and library research about the different attitudes people have about hair. Make a picture book of these stories and sayings.

| ⊙ R | ⊙ U | ⊙ Ap |
| ○ An | ○ E | ○ C |

20. Continued from Activity 19

Find out how people's attitudes toward hair and haircuts for men and women have changed over the centuries. Research as far back as you can. Compare modern ideas to other periods in history. Look also at the social revolution of the 1960s and how people used hair as a symbol of change. Make a diagram to show these changes.

| ⊙ R | ⊙ U | ⊙ Ap |
| ⊙ An | ○ E | ○ C |

21. Cajun legend

Jean Sot is the main figure in a series of stories about luck and foolishness. What does his name mean? Find stories about Jean Sot. Develop one of your own where his foolishness influences luck. Here are two possible sources:
- *The Rainbow Book of American Folk Tales and Legends*
- *The Luck Book*

Both are written and compiled by Maria Leach.

⊙ R	⊙ U	○ Ap
⊙ An	○ E	⊙ C

22. Foxfire

The *Foxfire Books* are a series compiled by a group of secondary school English students in America. They talked with native Appalachians about their beliefs. These have been collected and recorded. Do the same for your area. Talk to older people about their superstitions and beliefs. Compile your own cultural foxfire type book. Give it an appropriate name.

○ R	○ U	○ Ap
⊙ An	○ E	⊙ C

23. Lucky numbers

Both 7 and 13 are related to beliefs of good luck and bad luck. Why are they said to be lucky or unlucky? Find examples of beliefs dealing with both numbers. Make a chart of lucky and unlucky beliefs relating to these numbers. What other information do you find relating to luck and numbers?

○ R	⊙ U	⊙ Ap
⊙ An	○ E	○ C

24. Body magic

It is said that certain parts of the body are indicators of things that are happening or about to happen. What are these signs of?
- Your hand itches
- Your ears ring
- Your ears burn
- Your nose itches

Where did these beliefs originate? Add other examples to the list that you find.

○ R	⊙ U	⊙ Ap
○ An	○ E	○ C

93   *Don't teach! Let me learn!* HB6487

25. Lightning strikes

It is said that lightning never strikes twice in the same place. Is this fact or superstition? How might this idea have developed? Make a list of lightning-related folklore, and the scientific evidence that either proves or disproves them.

O R	⊙ U	O Ap
⊙ An	⊙ E	O C

26. Jiminy cricket

In the movie *Pinocchio*, Jiminy Cricket sings the song, *When You Wish Upon a Star*. Find the music and listen to it. What other star-related wishes and charms can you find? What are your own beliefs about wishing on stars? Have you ever wished on a shooting star?

⊙ R	⊙ U	⊙ Ap
⊙ An	O E	O C

27. Mandragora

Find out about as many plants (flowers or herbs) that are associated with different powers as you can. Make a chart of their healing or destructive effects. Include illustrations. Is there any scientific evidence to support belief in these powers?

⊙ R	⊙ U	⊙ Ap
O An	O E	⊙ C

28. Evil spirits

Some people wear an asafoetida bag. What is it? What is it supposed to do? Do you think it works? Why? Make one and try it out yourself? What are your results?. What other objects are believed to ward off evil spirits? Ask people you know if they carry anything to bring good luck, or to ward off bad luck.

O R	⊙ U	O Ap
⊙ An	⊙ E	⊙ C

29. Kill or cure

Garlic is said to have the power to ward off evil spirits. It also is thought to have medicinal value. Research this plant. Find out about its supposed powers and also about its popular uses. Do people still believe in these powers today? Write a report.

O R	⊙ U	O Ap
⊙ An	O E	⊙ C

30. Jinxed!

What is a jinx? The Hope Diamond and the Pharaoh's Curse are two of the best known. What are their stories? What evidence do you have that either or both may be true? Not true? Have you ever felt jinxed? Explain.

O R	⊙ U	O Ap
⊙ An	⊙ E	⊙ C

31. Magic squares

Magic squares are groups of numbers that result in the same total no matter which direction they are added. These were thought to have magical powers and were incorporated into jewellery by some cultures. Create a magic square for yourself. Does it work mathematically? Does it improve your luck?

O R	⊙ U	⊙ Ap
⊙ An	⊙ E	O C

32. Horoscopes

Many people believe that horoscopes are indicators of what will happen. On what is your horoscope based? Do you read your horoscope each day? Is it a good predictor? According to your horoscope, what are your lucky and unlucky days? What is the prediction process that makes it appropriate/inappropriate for each person?

⊙ R	⊙ U	O Ap
⊙ An	⊙ E	O C

33. Holiday superstitions

What superstitions are associated with these holidays? How do these superstitions affect the customs and activities of your family?

• All-Souls' Day
• St Patrick's Day
• Valentine's Day
• Halloween
• New Year's Day
• Christmas

What ideas are these superstitions based on? Where does the word 'holiday' come from?

⊙ R	⊙ U	○ Ap
⊙ An	⊙ E	○ C

34. Mirror, mirror on the wall

Many people hold strong beliefs about mirrors and other reflective surfaces. Find out about as many of these beliefs from different cultures as you can. Make a list of these attitudes and compare cultures. Why do you think these beliefs are so strongly held?

⊙ R	⊙ U	⊙ Ap
○ An	⊙ E	○ C

35. Superstition and culture

Anthropologist Margaret Mead reports that superstition has been a part of every civilised culture. Would you agree with Dr Mead? Choose two or three cultural groups (present or past). Investigate to find superstitious beliefs that influence people's lives. Make a chart to show similarities and uniquenesses.

○ R	⊙ U	○ Ap
⊙ An	⊙ E	⊙ C

36. Symbols of superstition

Some symbols are associated with superstition and beliefs. Research to find their meaning or significance and the basis for it. Can you add other symbols? Develop a chart showing the symbol, its meaning and its source or origin.

○ R	⊙ U	⊙ Ap
⊙ An	○ E	⊙ C

Monsters

Monsters

Activity	Remembering	Understanding	Applying	Analysing	Evaluating	Creating
1	x	x				
2	x	x				
3				x		x
4	x					
5	x	x				
6				x		x
7	x	x				
8				x	x	
9		x		x	x	
10				x	x	x
11				x		x
12	x	x	x			
13	x	x				
14	x	x	x			
15		x		x		x
16	x	x		x		x
17		x		x	x	x
18		x		x		
19				x		x
20	x	x				

Monsters

Activity	Remembering	Understanding	Applying	Analysing	Evaluating	Creating
21	x	x	x			x
22		x	x			
23		x	x			x
24	x	x	x			
25		x	x			
26				x		x
27				x	x	x
28	x	x				
29	x	x				
30	x	x	x	x		x
31	x	x				
32	x			x	x	
33					x	
34		x	x			
35	x	x				
36		x		x		
37			x	x		x
38				x	x	x
39	x	x	x	x		
40				x	x	x

1. Definition

Monster comes from the Latin word that means 'to warn'. Compare this origin with dictionary entries. How does the meaning fit your idea of monsters?

⦿ R   ⦿ U   ○ Ap
○ An   ○ E   ○ C

2. Draco

Dragons are mythological beasts. What is the meaning of the term 'dragon'? What physical characteristics does a dragon usually possess?

⦿ R   ⦿ U   ○ Ap
○ An   ○ E   ○ C

3. Your own dragon

After studying various dragon representations in activity 4, create your own. Use your imagination to make the best dragon possible. Invite other classmates to contribute dragons of their own.

○ R   ○ U   ○ Ap
⦿ An   ○ E   ⦿ C

4. Dragon art

Artists depict dragons in a variety of ways. Using your library, make a collection of dragon pictures. You may wish to develop a noticeboard display showing these various dragons.

⦿ R   ○ U   ○ Ap
○ An   ○ E   ○ C

5. Dragon or dragoon

The military term 'dragoon' comes from the word 'dragon'. Explain how this transition was made.

⦿ R   ⦿ U   ○ Ap
○ An   ○ E   ○ C

6. Sea dragon

Some dragons are believed to live in the sea. Find out about the belief that sea dragons cause typhoons. Write this as a myth. Illustrate it.

○ R   ○ U   ○ Ap
⦿ An   ○ E   ⦿ C

7. Elephant man

In recent years the story of John Merrick was made into a movie called *The Elephant Man*. Merrick's sad story was told as his life unfolded. A carnival promotor exploited his abnormality. Research the life of Merrick. Explain the real problem and how he was misunderstood by others.

⦿ R	⦿ U	○ Ap
○ An	○ E	○ C

8. Tiny versus big

Both giants and dwarfs are considered in the monster category because of their odd size. In literature the giant is usually gentle, easily bullied and none too clever. On the other hand, dwarfs tend to be clever, witty and able to outsmart others. Read a variety of fairytales. Record your findings to prove or disprove this characterisation.

○ R	○ U	○ Ap
⦿ An	⦿ E	○ C

9. Sideshow freaks

In the days of the travelling circus, sideshows were common and popular with the people. Now these exploitations of humans are banned. Investigate to find some of the people who, because of their deformity, became famous. Make a collection of pictures, if possible. Why do you suppose these people participated in these shows? Why do you suppose people wanted to see them?

○ R	⦿ U	○ Ap
⦿ An	⦿ E	○ C

10. Sea monsters

A report in the *London Times*, October 1948, gives an account of a huge creature surfacing and passing near a sailing ship. Try to find this account or a portion of it. Is it true or fictitious? What did the sailors really see? How do you explain this sighting?

○ R	○ U	○ Ap
⦿ An	⦿ E	⦿ C

11. Animal or human?

Many mythological beasts combine the features of humans and one or more animals. You have seen some of these in your reading. Now design your own. Create the beast of all times. Illustrate or make a model. Include a description of where the beast lives, what it eats and how it behaves.

○ R   ○ U   ○ Ap
◉ An   ○ E   ◉ C

12. Triads

Research to find out what gorgons are. Where did they originate? How did the image of gorgons change over the years? What modern-day evidence is there of gorgon mythology? Create a chart to show the origin and evolution of gorgons. Include illustrations.

◉ R   ◉ U   ◉ Ap
○ An   ○ E   ○ C

13. Who were they?

Identify these mythical beasts. Decsribe what they looked like and give information about their origin, powers etc. You may wish to illustrate each.

- Satyrs
- Sphinxes
- Harpies
- Centaurs
- Hecafe
- Scylla

◉ R   ◉ U   ○ Ap
○ An   ○ E   ○ C

14. Centaur monsters

In the book *Gulliver's Travels* by Jonathan Swift, there are two groups of centaur monsters matched against each other. What were the two groups? Make a chart to show physical and performance characteristics of each. Include a picture of each on your chart.

◉ R   ◉ U   ◉ Ap
○ An   ○ E   ○ C

15. Fraidy cat

In the book *Clyde Monster* by Robert L. Crowe, the young monster is afraid of the dark. Consider this. Think of a monster you have read about or created. Consider the monster as a baby. Write a baby monster story of your own.

| ○ R | ◉ U | ○ Ap |
| ◉ An | ○ E | ◉ C |

16. Penny dreadfuls

During the mid 1800s in England a new literature type appeared on the market in London. It was known as 'bloods' or penny dreadful. Find out about this literature type. Why was it popular? Try to write your own 'penny dreadful'.

| ◉ R | ◉ U | ○ Ap |
| ◉ An | ○ E | ◉ C |

17. Hitchcock monsters

Alfred Hitchcock is associated with some rather special mystery stories. He also edited a book called the *Monster Museum*. Take a look at it. Perhaps you can create your own Monster Museum in the classroom. Label each display as it would be in a real museum. Who will be included?

| ○ R | ◉ U | ○ Ap |
| ◉ An | ◉ E | ◉ C |

18. Monster ideas

Frankenstein was created by Mary Wollstonecraft Shelly. She developed the story around the work of a young German scientist whose purpose was not to create a monster at all. Read the story. What was the real intent? How did the Frankenstein accident occur? Why do you think this story has become a horror classic?

| ○ R | ◉ U | ○ Ap |
| ◉ An | ○ E | ○ C |

19. A future look

Mermaids and their offspring are said to have the gift of prophecy. As oracles they can, it is said, predict the future. If you were to receive a prediction from a mermaid, what would it be?

○ R	○ U	○ Ap
⦿ An	○ E	⦿ C

20. Mermaid mania

What are mermaids? What qualities are they said to have? Are there mermen? Research through reading and pictures to find out about this strange creature. Clue: Norwegian legends may be helpful.

⦿ R	⦿ U	○ Ap
○ An	○ E	○ C

21. A look at the picture

Lewis Carroll once said, when asked to define a griffin, 'If you don't know what a griffin is, look at the picture'. Make a picture book of monsters. Include captions for each picture.

⦿ R	⦿ U	⦿ Ap
○ An	○ E	⦿ C

22. Super monsters

Many of the super monsters were created specifically for films. Make a monster list and develop a research chart or timeline to show when the monster was created and for what film.

○ R	⦿ U	⦿ Ap
○ An	○ E	⦿ C

23. A pet

In Peggy Parrish's book *No More Monsters For Me*, a monster pet has caused some problems. Read the book. Using puppets, act out one of the best scenes.

○ R	⦿ U	⦿ Ap
○ An	○ E	⦿ C

24. Invisible monsters

The bunyip is one example of an invisible monster. Find out about the bunyip (of course, there are no pictures!). Write a description. What other invisible monsters can you identify?

⦿ R	⦿ U	⦿ Ap
○ An	○ E	○ C

25. Movie monsters

Think about the monster or horror movies you have seen. Make a list of movie monsters. Take each of these and develop a character traits chart. Include both physical and personality traits. For example:

Monster	Physical Traits	Character Traits
Godzilla	lizard-like, huge, small head	mean, destructive, frightened

⊙ R   ⊙ U   ⊙ Ap
○ An   ○ E   ○ C

---

26. Monster care

Suppose that a large box is delivered to your house. You open it and inside is a baby monster. The note says you may keep it and care for it. What does the baby look like? What are the care instructions? Illustrate a *How To Care for the Monster* book. Give your monster a name.

○ R   ○ U   ○ Ap
⊙ An   ○ E   ⊙ C

---

27. Choose one

Select one of these monsters or monster types. Research its origin and history. Develop a historical research presentation. Use visuals if appropriate. Based on your research, does (or did) the monster exist? Explain your answer.
- Lochness Monster
- Vampire
- Dragon
- Werewolf
- Abominable Snowman
- Cyclops

○ R   ○ U   ○ Ap
⊙ An   ⊙ E   ⊙ C

28. Dead or alive?

What is a vampire like? It is said a vampire is 'undead'. What does this mean? Explain how this state enables the monster to behave in unique ways.

⊙ R	⊙ U	○ Ap
○ An	○ E	○ C

29. Count dracula

The Count is one of the most famous modern monsters. Who was the actor that developed the character of Dracula? Who was the writer or creator of the story? Find out about the lives of these two men.

⊙ R	⊙ U	○ Ap
○ An	○ E	○ C

30. Which face?

A werewolf is a monster that changes in physical appearance. Draw before and after pictures of a werewolf. Are werewolves real? Where did this belief originate? What do you think?

⊙ R	⊙ U	⊙ Ap
⊙ An	○ E	⊙ C

31. Real or imaginary?

Some monsters (vampires particularly) are said to come from Transylvania. Is Transylvania a real place or not? Explain your answer.

⊙ R	⊙ U	○ Ap
○ An	○ E	○ C

32. Greatest monster

St George is said to have slain the 'greatest monster of all time'. What was the monster? Do you agree that it was the greatest? Explain.

⊙ R	○ U	○ Ap
⊙ An	⊙ E	○ C

33. Fears and fables

Why do you think people have always believed in monsters? Based on the information you have gathered so far, write an essay explaining your point of view.

○ R	○ U	○ Ap
○ An	⊙ E	○ Ap

34. Unicorns

When we think of the beautiful white horse-like animal, it does not seem to fall into the monster category; however, first accounts of unicorns were accounts of monsters and monstrous behaviour. Trace the development of the unicorn and the changes in its behaviour and appearance.

○ R	◉ U	◉ Ap
○ An	○ E	○ C

35. Living dead

Some monsters have been created based on the dead coming to life. Choose one or more of these and investigate their origin and development.

- Mummies
- Houngans
- Zombies
- Vampires

◉ R	◉ U	○ Ap
○ An	○ E	○ C

36. Monster's language

The word 'berserk' is part of our modern vocabulary. What does this word mean now? How did it develop? What was the origin of the word? How does its origin relate to its modern meaning? Make a list of other monster-related words.

○ R	◉ U	○ Ap
◉ An	○ E	○ C

37. Changes

Other monsters beside the werewolf change physical form. Make a list of those who change appearance. Using before and after pictures, develop a matching card-game memory. Play your game with some friends and see if they can name the monsters.

○ R	○ U	◉ Ap
◉ An	○ E	◉ C

38. Your account

You are travelling across the sea, captain of your ship. It is dark and stormy. On the horizon you see some strange shape. Write your account. Is it a monster? How do you know? How does it behave? Make it real to your readers.

○ R	○ U	○ Ap
◉ An	◉ E	◉ C

39. Purple people eaters

Strange monsters have been reported from outer space. These accounts show up in songs, books, movies etc. Make a scrapbook of extra-terrestrial monsters. Make a chart that ranks them in order from least scary to most scary.

◉ R	◉ U	◉ Ap
○ An	○ E	○ C

40. Monster award

You have been selected to design an award to be presented at the Best Monster of the Year convention. What will it look like? To whom will it be given? Show a picture of the monster and the award.

○ R	○ U	○ Ap
◉ An	◉ E	◉ C

Fantasy

Fantasy

Activity	Remembering	Understanding	Applying	Analyisng	Evaluating	Creating
1		x	x			
2		x		x		x
3	x	x	x		x	
4				x	x	x
5				x		x
6				x		x
7	x	x	x			
8	x	x	x			
9	x	x	x	x		x
10				x	x	x
11		x		x	x	x
12	x	x	x			
13				x		x
14				x		x
15		x	x			
16		x		x		x
17				x		x
18				x	x	
19				x		x

Fantasy

Activity	Remembering	Understanding	Applying	Analyisng	Evaluating	Creating
20				x		x
21				x	x	
22				x		x
23				x		x
24				x		x
25	x	x	x			
26				x		x
27				x		x
28		x		x		
29				x		x
30				x	x	x
31				x		x
32		x		x	x	
33				x		x
34				x		x
35				x	x	x
36		x		x	x	
37	x	x	x			x
38	x	x		x	x	

Fantasy

1. Reality or fantasy?

Sometimes the truth is stranger than fiction. Scan the *Guinness Book of World Records*.
Make a chart of facts that seem fantastic! What intrigued you about these facts?

| O R | ◉ U | ◉ Ap |
| O An | O E | O C |

Fantasy

2. When you were small

Did you ever pretend things when you were small? Perhaps you had an imaginary friend or pet. Maybe some room had strange powers or an object behaved in an unusual way. Write about your pretend experiences.

| O R | ◉ U | O Ap |
| ◉ An | O E | ◉ C |

Fantasy

3. Little folk

In *Peter Pan*, Peter never wants to grow up. Find characters in other stories who do or who want to stay young forever. Make a list. Why would these characters not want to be grown up?

| ◉ R | ◉ U | ◉ Ap |
| O An | ◉ E | O C |

Fantasy

4. Boo!

Have you ever been scared? Think back to your experience. Describe a time you remember being frightened. How did it all work out? What really happened?

| O R | O U | O Ap |
| ◉ An | ◉ E | ◉ C |

Fantasy

5. The joke's on you

Perhaps you have had this experience. Have you ever tried to play a joke or trick on someone else only to have it backfire on you? Describe it.

| O R | O U | O Ap |
| ◉ An | O E | ◉ C |

Fantasy

6. Magic travel

Magic cars have been the centre of some feature films and books. Perhaps you have read or can read *Chitty Chitty Bang Bang* or *Herbie the Love Bug*. Suppose your family car could fly, or better yet, your bicycle. What then?

| O R | O U | O Ap |
| ◉ An | O E | ◉ C |

7. Fantasy in literature

Read to find ways that authors use fantasy devices. Make a chart or picture collection of these. For example, Aladdin had a magic lamp and Wonder Woman had an invisible plane that she could fly in. What were the other devices you found?

⊙ R	⊙ U	⊙ Ap
O An	O E	O C

8. The magic of it all

Merlin is probably the most famous of all magicians. Investigate the world of real magicians. Develop a magical 'Who's Who'. Include the magicians and the illusion or feat for which they were best known. Include both real and fanciful magicians.

⊙ R	⊙ U	⊙ Ap
O An	O E	O C

9. May the force be with you

The *Star Wars* fantasy has become important to many of us over the last few years. The 'force' has influenced movies, toys, clothing and other aspects of our lives. Make a *Star Wars* scrapbook showing the influence of fantasy on real life.

⊙ R	⊙ U	⊙ Ap
⊙ An	O E	⊙ C

10. Just suppose

All of a sudden you have magical powers. You can do something no one else can do or something totally unexpected.
What power do you have? How does this affect the way you look? The way you act? The way others treat you?

O R	O U	O Ap
⊙ An	⊙ E	⊙ C

11. Rose-coloured glasses

Fantasy

It is said that some people see the world through 'rose-coloured glasses'. What does this expression mean? Suppose you found a pair of 'rose-coloured glasses'. Write a story to tell how the world would be as you see it.

○ R	⊙ U	○ Ap
⊙ An	⊙ E	⊙ C

12. Believe it or not

Fantasy

For years a gentleman named Ripley collected unusual information for a newspaper column called, 'Believe It or Not'. These have been compiled into books of strange information. Find some examples of 'Believe It or Not'. Develop a Believe It or Not noticeboard for the class. Try to pick really hard-to-believe items.

⊙ R	⊙ U	⊙ Ap
○ An	○ E	○ C

13. 13th hour

Fantasy

In the book *Tom's Midnight Garden* by A. Philippa Pearce, Tom thinks he hears the clock strike – thirteen times! It wakes him and he finds the house is transformed into a fantasy world. Think about a 13th hour. What might happen to you? Write a story about your experiences in your 13th hour.

○ R	○ U	○ Ap
⊙ An	○ E	⊙ C

14. Ghostly residence

Fantasy

Many fantasy stories have unusual or mysterious settings. Often these include a haunted house. Make a drawing, diorama or model of the best haunted house you can design. Write a description of your house that would create a mythical setting for a super spooky story.

○ R	○ U	○ Ap
⊙ An	○ E	⊙ C

15. Transformationally speaking

Authors of fantasy stories often start the narrative with normal events and characters. At some point something happens to transform the character or events into fantasy. Some examples would be Dr Jekyll to Mr Hyde and the transformation to The Incredible Hulk. What are some other transformations? Make a list of stories that begin normally and are transformed to fantasy.

O R	⊙ U	⊙ Ap
O An	O E	O C

16. Author style

An author's word choice is an important tool used to create illusions in the reader's mind. Consider how you might use analogies and expand descriptions of these story events. Rewrite each to be vividly descriptive. Add others.
- A squeaking door
- Someone groaning
- Chairs rattling
- Wind blowing
- Stairs creaking
- Someone snoring

O R	⊙ U	O Ap
⊙ An	O E	⊙ C

17. Time machine

In Lloyd Alexander's book *Time Cat* the main character, through the magical powers of his cat, can travel in time and space. Pretend you have stumbled on a time machine. Get inside. Push the button.

Describe your experiences.

O R	O U	O Ap
⊙ An	O E	⊙ C

18. The midas touch

King Midas had the power to change things he touched to gold. At first he was thrilled with this ability. Then he found it created problems. Suppose everything you touched turned to chocolate. How would this change your life? Would you like the change or not?

Explain your feelings.

O R	O U	O Ap
⊙ An	⊙ E	O C

19. Write now

Fantasy

Suppose you were developing a King Midas type character. Give your character a magic touch. Use the story of King Midas as a model and write a new Midas type story.

O R	O U	O Ap
⊙ An	O E	⊙ C

20. Attic antics

Fantasy

Some mysterious creature lives in your roof. You've been hearing noises and noticed some strange events. You've become really brave! You're climbing up to the roof to see what's going on. You open the door and there it is! Describe the creature you find.

O R	O U	O Ap
⊙ An	O E	⊙ C

21. The mind's eye

Fantasy

Close your eyes and create a mini-picture of an exciting place you'd like to visit. Take some time and create details in your picture. Now, using your art skills, draw the scene you visualise.

O R	O U	O Ap
⊙ An	⊙ E	O C

22. Guess who?

Fantasy

Halloween is a time for fantasy and imagination. Dream up your ideal costume. Draw a picture of yourself in your costume. Add details so that it is exactly as you see it in your mind. Be sure no one recognises you.

O R	O U	O Ap
⊙ An	O E	⊙ C

23. It's a tall tale

Fantasy

Tall tales are a form of fantasy story. Find out about the story of Lassiter's Reef. Create a new tall tale and put your own character in the story.

O R	O U	O Ap
⊙ An	O E	⊙ C

24. The rainbow's end

Fantasy

There is a legend that tells us that a pot of gold is to be found at the 'end of the rainbow'. Suppose it's true. You know because you find it. Tell us what happens.

O R	O U	O Ap
⊙ An	O E	⊙ C

Fantasy

25. Super power

In fantasy stories, people can often do strange or unusual things. They may be able to fly, have super-human strength or change appearance. Make a picture display of super heroes and fantasy characters. Label each with their super powers. For example: Mary Poppins – flies.

⦿ R ⦿ U ⦿ Ap
○ An ○ E ○ C

Fantasy

26. Fantasy or reality?

Sometimes, fantasy at one time becomes reality in another time period. Consider the stories by Jules Verne, 2001 and the Buck Rogers fantasy. Make a list to show what elements of the stories were fantasy when the stories were written. Tick any of these elements that have become reality over the years. Add other stories to your chart.

⦿ R ⦿ U ⦿ Ap
○ An ○ E ○ C

Fantasy

27. Flubber-gasting

Some years ago a movie was developed about a very special basketball team. One of the characters developed a rubber substance with magical bouncing powers call 'flubber'. With flubber on their shoes, the team could out-jump and out-run evryone else. Put some flubber on your shoes with your imagination. Tell about your flubber-gasting experiences.

○ R ○ U ○ Ap
⦿ An ○ E ⦿ C

Fantasy

28. Fantasy to reality

Flash Gordon was a fantasy cartoon character. Using the library, find out about the fantasy feats of Flash Gordon when the comic strip was newly developed. Which of his special abilities or skills has become a reality? How has science changed the image of Flash Gordon?

○ R ⦿ U ○ Ap
⦿ An ○ E ○ C

Fantasy

29. Down a rabbit hole

Lewis Carroll's Alice fell down a hole and found herself in Wonderland. Suppose you have gone for a walk near your home. You feel yourself slipping – falling – out of control. Write about your new surroundings and your adventures there.

O R   O U   O Ap
⊙ An   O E   ⊙ C

Fantasy

30. Unpredictable characters

In fantasy stories things often happen that can't happen in reality. Develop a unique character for a fantasy story. Make your character from something unique. For example, it might be an animal or an inanimate object that can talk and/or walk.

O R   O U   O Ap
⊙ An   O E   ⊙ C

Fantasy

31. Point of view

In some situations people see things differently. The point of view of the person sometimes colours or affects the fantasy. Consider a story such as *Cinderella*. What was the fantasy element? How might the story have been told from the prince's knowledge and viewpoint? Be the prince. Retell the story.

O R   O U   O Ap
⊙ An   ⊙ E   ⊙ C

Fantasy

32. War of the worlds

Orson Welles produced a radio drama by this name in the 1940s. It was based on a novel by H.G. Wells and it was so real that listeners believed the story to be true. Find a recording of this broadcast at a library. Listen to it. Record elements and techniques that were used to make it seem real.

O R   ⊙ U   O Ap
⊙ An   ⊙ E   O C

Fantasy

33. An alien view

Suppose a creature from another planet were to drop in on you. The creature is going to watch and report behaviours. Write an alien's report describing your bedroom, or your school, or a sport you play.
Remember the alien will have to use their imagination.

○ R	○ U	○ Ap
◉ An	○ E	◉ C

Fantasy

34. Bionics

Some years ago a television series featured characters who had been equipped with bionic devices. These bionics gave them super human powers. Suppose you had an organ or limb transplant and bionic parts were accidentally implanted. What powers would you have? How would it affect your life?

○ R	○ U	○ Ap
◉ An	○ E	◉ C

Fantasy

35. Invisible characters

In the movie *Harvey*, one of the main characters was an invisible rabbit. In the TV show *Topper*, a ghost was invisible. The only thing that you could see was his top hat and cane. Imagine that you have the power to be invisible. What kind of mischief can you get into? What problems could you create or solve? Write a story in which the main character is invisible. Make it believable.

○ R	○ U	○ Ap
◉ An	◉ E	◉ C

Fantasy

36. Magical beings

Some story characters are fantasy characters. Take for example, the unicorn. Research to find out about this fanciful beast. Is there any basis for believing the unicorn is real? Explain.

○ R	◉ U	○ Ap
◉ An	◉ E	○ C

37. Personality development

An author may develop a fantasy character by taking a personality and exaggerating it. Try your hand at developing some exaggerated personalities. Here are some starters.

He's so slow that he _____

She's so dumb that she _____

He's so clumsy that he _____

She's so clever that she _____

⊙ R	⊙ U	⊙ Ap
○ An	○ E	⊙ C

38. Mythology

The gods, goddesses and beasts of mythology are fanciful characters. Make a chart to show mythological creatures. After listing them, show what characters were fantasy and which were real.

Characters	Fanciful traits	Real traits

⊙ R	⊙ U	○ Ap
⊙ An	⊙ E	○ C

Student independent study project

Goals: _____
_____
_____

What I hope to learn: _____
_____
_____

Procedure to follow: _____
_____
_____

Research I intend to do: _____
_____
_____

Bibliography: _____
_____
_____

Activities I intend to do: _____
_____
_____

Materials I need: _____
_____
_____

Target date for completion: _____
Final presentation to include: _____
_____
_____

Student signature: _____
Teacher signature: _____
Parent signature: _____

Student work log

Week I: Monday   _____
                Tuesday   _____
                Wednesday _____
                Thursday _____
                Friday _____
                Teacher conference – Needs: _____
                                    Completions: _____
                                    Comments: _____

Week II: Monday   _____
                Tuesday   _____
                Wednesday _____
                Thursday _____
                Friday _____
                Teacher conference – Needs: _____
                                    Completions: _____
                                    Comments: _____

Week III: Monday   _____
                Tuesday   _____
                Wednesday _____
                Thursday _____
                Friday _____
                Teacher conference – Needs: _____
                                    Completions: _____
                                    Comments: _____

Completion week:

_____ Research reports properly written; proofread; rewritten.

_____ Activities completed.

_____ Unit organised.

_____ Presentation prepared.

This is a sample form for students' organisation of study skills.

The student–teacher conference is very important on a regular basis for needs assessment as well as for constant evaluation and supervision.